CUCINARE

Healthy and Authentic Italian Cooking
for the Whole Family

Published in 2020 by
Harper Design
An Imprint of HarperCollins *Publishers*
195 Broadway
New York, NY 10007
Tel: (212) 207-7000
Fax: (855) 746-6023
harperdesign@harpercollins.com
www.hc.com

Distributed throughout the world by
HarperCollins *Publishers*
195 Broadway
New York, NY 10007

ISBN 978-0-06-295883-9

Printed in Singapore

First printing, 2020

MARCO BIANCHI

{ CUCINARE }

Healthy and Authentic Italian Cooking for the Whole Family

HARPER
DESIGN

An Imprint of HarperCollinsPublishers

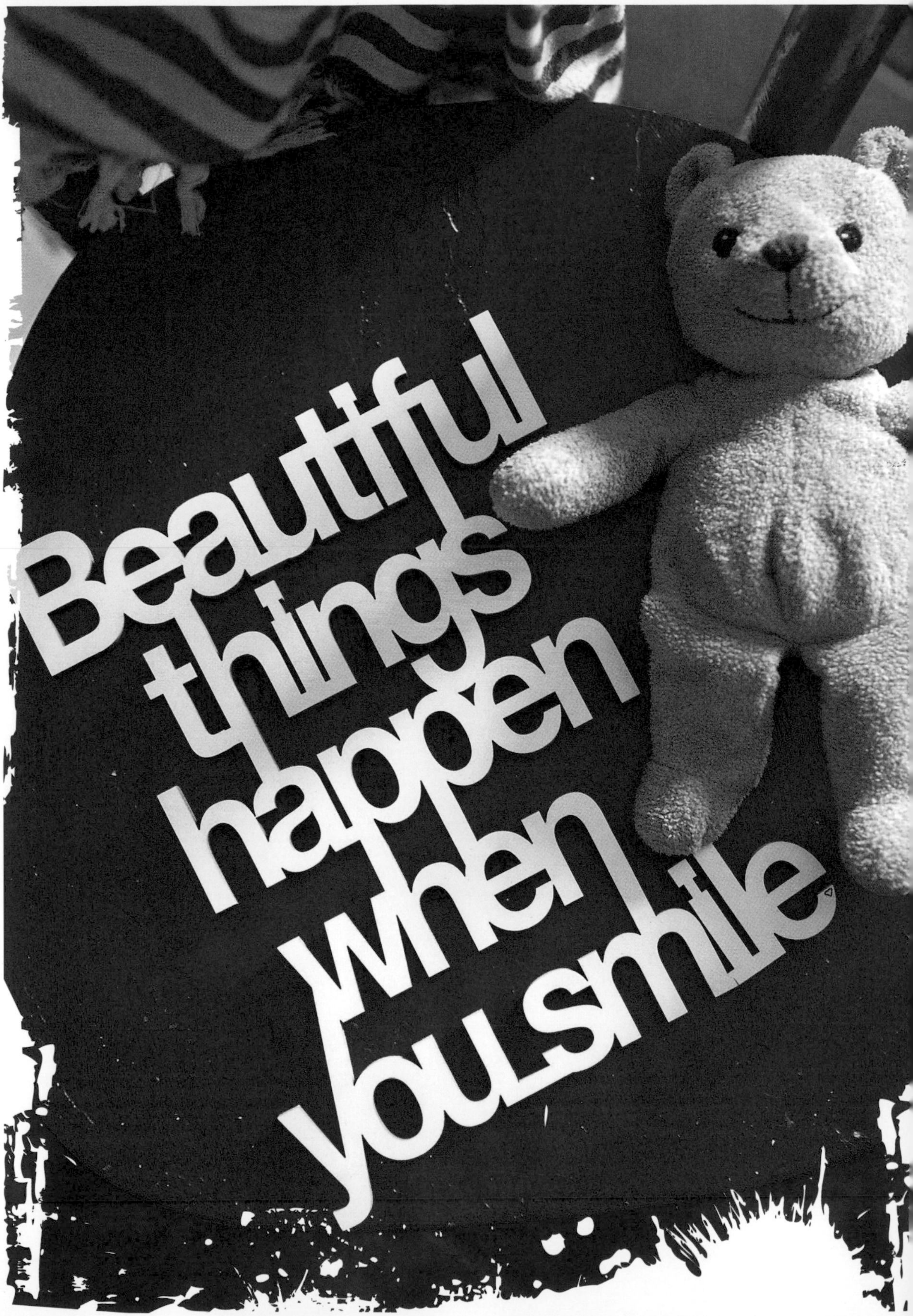
Beautiful
things
happen
when
you smile

 # CONTENTS

Welcome! —————————————————————— 11

Cooking Is . . . ——————————————————— 14

Operating Instructions ——————————————— 17

10 Things I Do for Better Health ————————— 19

Basket No. 1 ——————————————————— **41**

Eggless Mayonnaise + Variations ——————— 43

#tasteandhealth ———————————————— 44

Crispy Anchovies with Lemon ———————— 45

Pan de Mej + Variations —————————— 46

#tasteandhealth ———————————————— 48

Green Toasts ——————————————————— 49

Falafel ——————————————————————— 51

Basket No. 2 _____ **53**

#tasteandhealth _____ 54

Lentil and Walnut Salad _____ 55

Granola _____ 56

Kisses + Variation _____ 59

Apple-Walnut Salad with
Balsamic-Honey Dressing _____ 60

#tasteandhealth _____ 61

Ricotta Berry Tartlets + Variations _____ 63

Pancakes with Bananas,
Raspberries, and Honey _____ 64

#tasteandhealth _____ 66

Crumble + Variations _____ 67

Basket No. 3 _____ **69**

Savory Leek Tart + Variation _____ 70

Eggless Leek Frittata _____ 73

Pumpkin Soup with Ginger + Variation _____ 74

#tasteandhealth _____ 75

Pumpkin and Chickpea Spread _____ 77

Pea, Zucchini, and Goat Cheese Pesto
+ Variation _____ 78

#tasteandhealth _____ 80

Greek Chickpea and Zucchini "Meatballs"
+ Variations _____ 81

Mediterranean Sushi _____ 82

Basket No. 4 — 85

Beet Chips — 86

Beet Cake — 87

Hummus + Variation — 88

#tasteandhealth — 90

Chickpea, Celery, and Feta Salad + Variations — 91

Avocado Tartare with Lime and Red Onion — 92

Celery, Apple, and Ginger Juice
+ Alternative — 95

Basket No. 5 — 97

Carrot-Yogurt Shots + Variation — 98

Chocolate Roll — 101

Individual Chocolate Lava Cakes + Variations — 102

#tasteandhealth — 103

Coconut Treats + Variations — 104

Carrot Muffins + Variation — 107

Pasta with Eggplant, Taggiasca Olives,
Capers, and Mint — 108

#tasteandhealth — 109

Matcha Crêpes — 110

Basket No. 6 — 113

Cannellini and Tuna "Meatballs" + Variations — 115

Gingerbread Men — 116

Barley Risotto-Style with Pepper and
Goat Cheese Cream + Variation — 119

#tasteandhealth ⎯⎯⎯⎯⎯ 120

Mini Focaccia Breads with Seeds and Olives ⎯⎯ 121

Stuffed Cabbage with Cannellini Puree ⎯⎯⎯ 122

Pan dei Morti Cookies ⎯⎯⎯⎯⎯ 125

Basket No. 7 ⎯⎯⎯⎯⎯⎯⎯ **127**

Home-Style Cake + Variation ⎯⎯⎯⎯ 129

Pea and Mint Mousse on Toast + Variations ⎯⎯ 130

#tasteandhealth ⎯⎯⎯⎯⎯ 132

Tube Cake with Yogurt Sauce + Variation ⎯⎯ 133

Roasted Cherry Tomatoes with Onions
+ Variation ⎯⎯⎯⎯⎯⎯⎯ 134

Pasta with Arugula Pesto and
Crispy Salmon + Variation ⎯⎯⎯⎯⎯ 137

#tasteandhealth ⎯⎯⎯⎯⎯ 138

#tasteandhealth ⎯⎯⎯⎯⎯ 139

Pizza + Variation ⎯⎯⎯⎯⎯⎯ 140

Mediterranean Bruschetta ⎯⎯⎯⎯ 143

Basket No. 8 ⎯⎯⎯⎯⎯⎯⎯ **145**

Tagliatelle with Mushrooms
and Ricotta-Pumpkin Cream ⎯⎯⎯⎯ 147

Seasonal Autumn Quinoa ⎯⎯⎯⎯ 148

Lentil Salad ⎯⎯⎯⎯⎯⎯⎯ 149

Cauliflower Pasta + Variations ⎯⎯⎯⎯ 150

#tasteandhealth ⎯⎯⎯⎯⎯ 151

Extra-Light Apple Cake ⎯⎯⎯⎯⎯ 153

Cream of Cauliflower, Celery Root, and
Greek Yogurt Soup _____ 154

#tasteandhealth _____ 156

Green Pasta _____ 157

Basket No. 9 _____ **159**

Classic Gazpacho + Alternative _____ 160

#tasteandhealth _____ 162

Apricot and Mango Salad _____ 163

Buckwheat Noodles Trapani-Style _____ 164

Cucumber Water + Variations _____ 167

Ricotta Spoon Sweet _____ 168

Apricot Cake _____ 169

Detox Juice _____ 170

Basket No. 10 _____ **173**

Black Rice with Lentils _____ 174

#tasteandhealth _____ 176

Pasta with Radicchio Sauce + Variation _____ 177

Farro and Chickpea Soup + Variation _____ 178

Radicchio and Apple Salad _____ 180

Farro Blancmange + Variation _____ 181

Radicchio Stuffed with Tofu and
Anchovy Mousse + Variation _____ 182

Thank You! _____ 185

Index by Dish _____ 186

Index by Ingredient _____ 190

WELCOME!

To me, cooking is an act of love—love of ourselves, the people we love, and all we hold dear. Even talking about food and health is, in my opinion, a way of expressing that love. The book that you are holding in your hands is dedicated to all of you—those who have followed me for years and demonstrate their affection for me every day, and those who have just decided to purchase it out of curiosity. You will find a lot of recipes in these pages, of course, but you'll find more, too: tips for wellness, health advice, some tricks to use in the kitchen, and lots of snapshots of moments in my own daily life.

I aimed to use this book to illustrate a new phase in my life and my career, and I want all of you to be a part of it! My goal remains the same: to promote the rules of good nutrition in my own way, with simple, direct language that begins with a foundation built on science and ends with your tables filled with natural, healthy food—with a lot of fun along the way.

Before I begin, I'd like to put a few things out there. Recently, as I've chatted with people in real life or on social media, I am frequently asked what reasons underlie my diet choices. They're enthusiastic and curious.

My first answer is that I have one rule: There is no single food that can be considered "poison" in and of itself. It all depends on the quantity and quality and on our subjective attitudes. We all take in nutrients from food in the same way.

That's why it's important to talk about science and research and data— even though, I will admit, data isn't always easy to interpret. Data may be murky and inaccessible, and that's why I always try to answer questions as clearly and pleasantly as possible, giving practical advice that can be applied in everyday life. We need to learn to eat not just with our stomachs, but also with our heads. That may sound difficult and boring, monotonous, and even trivial, but I promise you it is not. Eating with your head means learning to respect food, ingredients, and the planet where we live.

On that subject, I naturally cannot help but mention Professor Umberto Veronesi, whom I remember with affection and esteem. It's his "fault" that I am so determined to spread the word about science. I still remember when he told me, "Science is the most powerful tool humanity has to improve people's quality of life and perspective." Nothing truer nor more useful was ever spoken.

It all began with an email. I suggested a crazy project to him, and fewer than forty-eight hours later he called me to talk about it. This was in 2009. At the time I was a biochemistry research technician who simply wanted to go beyond the laboratory . . . He and I would go on to create a relationship of mutual respect, meetings, brainstorming, plans, and goals. Even though he was a very busy man, he was also accessible, funny, energetic, and very knowledgeable about everything—a true philosopher.

When a film director contacted him about a project related to vegetarians, he got me involved. Then, he invited me to contribute a piece to a book he was writing on nutrition. I asked him to be in the opening segment for my TV series and to write the foreword to one of my books, but I also invited him to be a guest at my wedding, because he was a man who I knew would have the right words at one of the most important moments in my life. After that, he asked me to stop addressing him as professor and use his first name, because we were family. I was never able to do it, however!

Each time we met, I was infused with positive energy and with a great desire to learn more, deepen my knowledge, and most of all to share that knowledge. "A researcher has to be curious and be hungry for knowledge," he often told me. "Keep going, because the world needs science and reason."

My friends, the fact that I am here today telling you about science as I do every day is something I owe solely to him. He was a man who taught me about life—a wonderful person who believed in my abilities and kept pushing me forward.

I hope that I have painted you a clear picture of my love for science, and that you will be tempted by the recipes in this book, but by including photos of my daily life, I also hope to impress upon you that to me living a free and conscious life is a choice: no labels, no obligation or requirement that you cook in one particular style.

I love nourishing myself this way, and I love cooking with my head for my family, my friends, and the other people I love, because cooking is the best way I know to express love.

COOKING IS . . .

Cooking is truly an act of love for ourselves and those around us. Even offering a recipe to a friend is a gesture of affection. It's a little like the way we interact on social media. That's why I wanted to include some of your thoughts in this book. (Though I have to say, it was really, really hard to choose the people to include!)

VALENTINA Cooking is an act of love . . . like caressing someone's heart. It's taking care of yourself and the people you love; that's why we cook with our hearts. It's consoling someone we love and lifting up someone when they're down. It's filling the kitchen with delicious smells that bring us back to our childhoods. It also can be a way to capture a person's heart. It means filling a plate with thousands of colors and still tasting simple flavors. Nursing a baby is the first act of love. Cooking brings us back to that time of warmth and joy.

BRUNA To me, cooking is a way to spend a half hour with my daughter, sweet and fragile Hikikomori, because she has to come out of her room—the comfort zone where she's been hiding out for the last four years—to eat.

MARCO Time in the kitchen is often spent waiting. In the kitchen we walk a sensory path toward beauty and we nourish our love. As the saying goes, "To wait is the infinitive of the verb 'to love.'"

GIULIA Cooking is letting go of all the tension, worry, and sadness, and, like magic, putting only joy, love, and happiness on the plate!

LAURA Cooking is a moment of healthy solitude, wonderful sharing, and deep understanding of others.

MATTEO Cooking is getting back in touch with nature and its smells and tastes. The taste of a dish is easily accessed and manipulated by big business, but there's always the flavor of the human hand, an experience that is infinitely more complex and permits food to bear the individual signature of those who cooked it, tended to it, thought about it, and its own special qualities. Taste cannot be falsified and requires time and effort. That taste is, basically, the taste of love.

SABRINA Cooking is mixing, cooking, and serving emotions.

MICHELA Cooking is care and love. My mother always cooked when she couldn't tell me how she felt in words; today I do the same with my family. In my kitchen sometimes there is fatigue and stress; other times there is joy and a love of life. What I mean is, look at what I'm cooking and you'll know how I feel today.

TINA Either you like cooking or you don't, because it's passion, love, ecstasy for the mind, the eyes, and the palate. I love creating things in the kitchen, especially for my family.

SILVANA Cooking is the thought of love, and I love.

SHARON As a child I played with my sister at guessing the ingredients in the dishes that our Iranian mother was making. And when something was particularly good, she told us, "There's a special ingredient that makes everything taste better—love." ♥

CINZIA If you "take care" of anyone in any way, you experience life day by day, moment by moment, and that care never feels wasted. One of the ways I take care of my loved ones is to cook, because cooking is a choice, a ritual, a gesture that makes me feel good. Cooking nourishes not only the body, but the soul.

Veru   Marco   Vivienne

OPERATING INSTRUCTIONS

This isn't your usual cookbook.

It doesn't contain any miracle diets.

It's not a memoir.

It's not a scientific encyclopedia.

This is a book about unbridled passion for good, healthy, practical cooking in the spot where the Mediterranean diet and preventive health meet and provide ideas about what to put on the table every day.

Ideas good for grown-ups and kids, for the whole family.

Let's imagine we're going grocery shopping. We purchase five or six items and then head home to cook something tasty. That's how to read this book: the ingredients chosen and photographed for each basket represent a base for a handful of recipes that don't waste one bit of what you've bought.

Obviously, in order to help you cook well and to use the ingredients in the baskets as best as possible, I'm starting with the presumption that you always—and I mean always—have certain ingredients in your pantry and your freezer, such as extra-virgin olive oil, cold-pressed organic corn and sunflower oil, whole-grain and partially whole-grain flours, various types of whole (or pearled) grains (including barley, farro, corn, quinoa, rice), onions, lemons, garlic, aromatic herbs (frozen are fine), tomato sauce, fat-free milk, various types of nondairy milk, and Greek yogurt.

Only when you have a fully equipped pantry will you be able to cook without making mistakes and also guarantee that you are healthy and that your palate is treated to great-tasting food with preventive power.

Every once in a while in this book you'll come across a page I have hashtagged #tasteandhealth. There you'll find factoids from the world of science (remember that my background is as a biochemistry research technician) and my years of lab work—especially my current position as scientific educator for the Fondazione Umberto Veronesi.

10 THINGS I DO FOR BETTER HEALTH

Here are the reasons behind some of the choices I make in the kitchen. Don't make the mistake of thinking that good taste and pleasure are not compatible with healthy eating.

Why do I choose whole-grain items? Why do I eat very little sugar? Why do I love extra-virgin olive oil so much?

The answers to these—and other—questions can be found in the following pages. I hope these answers will clear up any questions you have and provide clear explanations of scientific data in order to help you understand how easy it is to eat with your head in a healthy way.

Recommended
daily allowance
of salt

1

{ **Why do I limit salt and replace some of it with herbs and spices and always say to cook in "lightly salted water"?** }

It's simple! The average Italian man consumes more than 4,100 milligrams of sodium (about 1¾ teaspoons or 10.6 grams salt) per day, and the average Italian woman consumes nearly 3,200 milligrams sodium (about 1⅓ teaspoons or 8.2 grams salt). Both are nearly double the 2,000 milligrams sodium (about 1 teaspoon or 5 grams salt) suggested by the World Health Organization (WHO). It's important to find alternatives for flavoring your food. Too much salt causes hypertension, cardiovascular disease, obesity, osteoporosis, and cancer.

Why do I always specify "whole-grain" whenever possible?

Fiber is synonymous with good health, and getting a good daily dose of fiber in your diet protects you. Not only does fiber keep you regular, but it's also associated with lowering total cholesterol and LDL (that's "bad" cholesterol) and improving postprandial glycemia. Fiber is also a prebiotic: That means it selectively nurtures the growth and activity of intestinal micro-biota, lactobacillus and bifidobacteria, the "good" bacteria in our intestines. An active intestine is synonymous with a strong and capable immune system!

The recommended "dose" of fiber is 25 to 30 grams per day, according to WHO guidelines.

{ Why are my desserts less sweet than traditional treats? }

The WHO updated its guidelines for sugar consumption and strongly recommends cutting back so that sugar (meaning glucose, fructose, and table sugar) represents less than 10 percent of total daily intake. However, the WHO goes further and recommends that sugar actually represent less than 5 percent of daily intake (about 25 grams or 6 teaspoons). Indeed, sugar raises your blood sugar quickly and encourages inflammation and cell growth.

Since cells use sugar as their primary source of fuel, there is a theory that excess consumption of sugar may cause inflammation and growth of tumors, which means it can both increase the risk of getting sick and aggravate any existing disease.

Why do I choose some fats over others?

Extra-virgin olive oil (EVOO) helps keep your cardiovascular system young, strong, and healthy, because it contains good fats. It also fights tumors with polyphenols. And that's not all. This oil contains oleocanthal, a compound with anti-inflammatory properties that acts like a typical nonsteroidal anti-inflammatory. (That's what can make your throat burn slightly after you swallow extra-virgin olive oil.) EVOO is rich in polyphenols, so consuming it at every meal improves postprandial glycemia and the lipid profiles of those with prediabetes. All of these benefits are also found in nut and seed oils.

5

{ **Why do I include
so many vegetables
in every recipe?** }

Because we eat too few vegetables. We should be eating five servings of fruits and vegetables every day: two servings of vegetables and three of fruit, for a total of about 2 pounds (900 grams). Try to make your plate as colorful as possible by using a variety of ingredients. That way you'll take in plenty of minerals (potassium, magnesium, copper, zinc, calcium, iron, and so on), antioxidants (anthocyanins, lutein, flavonoids, and so on), and vitamins (A, C, E, folate, and more).

6

{ Why do I sometimes call for dairy milk and sometimes call for plant-based milks? }

Should you choose dairy milk (*vaccino*) or plant-based milks like soy (*soia*) and almond (*mandoria*)? Only you can answer that question. Are you lactose intolerant, allergic to milk, or diabetic, or are you subject to blood sugar swings or high cholesterol? Then you've probably already selected a type of milk that works for you. Always keep an eye on added sugar and the type of beverage. Rice milk is very starchy, for instance, and added sugar raises its glycemic index further; by comparison, fat-free milk as well as lactose-free fat-free milk have less impact on your body if consumed in line with the recommended daily allowance. Each recipe has a type of milk that works best, just as with individual palates and bodies. We don't all digest food the same way, so let's vary our diets. Your body will thank you!

Do you prefer soy, Greek, or dairy milk?

{ Why do I say you need to move a little each day? }

Moving consumes calories, but more important, it reduces the level of "bad" cholesterol (LDL) and raises the level of "good" cholesterol (HDL, or high-density lipoprotein, which carries excess cholesterol from tissues to the liver, which then works to remove it).

Walking lowers blood pressure and helps to control the risk of type 2 diabetes and of certain tumors that are influenced by hormonal activity, which can be stabilized through exercise.

I do CrossFit and functional fitness training, which combines aerobic and anaerobic exercise in a total workout that lasts less than a half hour.

Exercise makes us happy. Try it and you'll see!

{ Why don't I use 00 flour? }

The answer is simple: Italian "tipo 00" flour is the type of flour that offers the fewest benefits, because it's the most refined type. (The American equivalent is unbleached all-purpose flour.) As wheat is processed to make white flour, the most nutritious parts are removed. These include the germ, which is rich in vitamins, minerals, and amino acids, and the bran, which provides fiber. In the end, you're left with just starch, which is pure sugar. White flour doesn't do anything for your body; in fact, it raises the level of blood sugars.

Instead, use whole wheat flour, as it still contains all the nutrients, such as vitamins, minerals, and fiber.

In Italy, there are also a number of flours that fall in between refined white and whole wheat flours:

Tipo 0 flour: This is slightly less refined than "tipo 00" and contains a few parts of the bran and therefore has more fiber.

Tipo 1 flour: This falls in the middle of the range and has even more bran and fiber than tipo 0.

Tipo 2 flour: This is semi whole wheat flour and is a compromise between white flour and whole wheat flour.

Vary the
colors and flavors
you enjoy every day!

{ Why don't I cook (or eat) fresh meat or processed meat (cold cuts and preserved meat)? }

If you go over the weekly recommendation of a little over 1 pound (500 grams) of red meat (pork, beef, lamb, horse) or less than 2 ounces (50 grams) of processed meat, you increase your risk of cardiovascular disease and cancer—especially cancer of the gastrointestinal tract and especially rectal cancer, which is affected by the consumption and overeating of meat. This has been reported by the World Cancer Research Fund, which provides solid, reliable data.

What should you be eating instead? Legumes and grains, which provide a nutritionally complete meal. Legumes and grains are rich in vitamins (B1, B2, B3, B6, folate, and biotin) and protein and are the perfect replacement for animal protein sources.

10

{ Why am I always photographed barefoot and often with a cup of coffee in my hand? }

The answer to this is simple, too. Very simple. Ever since I was a kid I've walked barefoot at home and anywhere else that I could. (We don't grow out of all of our childhood habits.) I love to feel the ground beneath my feet without anything coming between us.

As for coffee, up to five or six espressos a day offer protection. Coffee is a friend to your arteries, because it's full of powerful antioxidants. Of course, this amount of caffeine might not be a good idea for people with certain health issues.

Coffee is also good for your liver, because it can prevent diseases such as cirrhosis, and it stops the formation of gallstones, which can be painful. And contrary to popular belief, caffeine has an analgesic effect: It's a vasoconstrictor. That means it narrows the blood vessels so that less blood flows through them—that makes it excellent for preventing headaches.

{ BASKET Nº 1 }

Finely Ground Cornmeal,
Fresh Anchovies,
Soy Milk,
Parsley,
Ground Turmeric,
Chickpeas

RECIPES

Eggless Mayonnaise + Variations _____ 43
Crispy Anchovies with Lemon _____ 45
Pan de Mej + Variations _____ 46
Green Toasts _____ 49
Falafel _____ 51

Eggless Mayonnaise

✓ **MAKES 1⅓ CUPS (300 GRAMS)**

¾ cup plus 2 tablespoons (220 ml) organic sunflower oil

¼ cup plus 3 tablespoons (100 ml) unsweetened soy milk

2 tablespoons apple cider vinegar or lemon juice

1 teaspoon mustard

½ teaspoon ground turmeric

Pinch of salt

In a container with high sides, combine all the ingredients. Mix with an immersion blender on high speed until dense and creamy.

This mayonnaise will keep in the refrigerator in a tightly sealed container for about 10 days.

Variations

1 Tuna

Drain 2 (4.5 oz/125 g) cans water-packed tuna. Flake into the mayonnaise after it is blended. Mix with a fork until combined.

2 Zing

Do you like a flavor punch? Add zest to your mayonnaise with cornichons and capers. Chop 5 cornichons and 1 tablespoon capers and fold them into the blended mayonnaise.

3 Spicy

Grate a ½-inch (1-cm) piece fresh ginger and add to the ingredients before blending into a mayonnaise.

4 Herbed

Mince 10 chives and the leaves of 2 sprigs of dill and add them to the mayonnaise after it is blended.

5 Pink

Add a chunk of cooked beet to the ingredients before blending the mayonnaise.

#tasteandhealth

Some nutrients are recommended to help combat inflammation. Among the most effective of these substances is a fatty acid called eicosapentaenoic acid (EPA), which yields the greatest anti-inflammatory effect when there is little arachidonic acid in the body. FATTY FISH have especially high levels of EPA.

Crispy Anchovies with Lemon

Ileana, the mother of my friend Andrea, first introduced me to this dish! You're going to love it. From sea to table, anchovies are a humble food, but really delicious. This dish is habit-forming: You've been warned!

SERVES 4

10½ ounces (300 g) cleaned fresh anchovies, boned and butterflied

2 to 3 tablespoons finely ground cornmeal

⅓ cup (50 g) pine nuts

Pinch of salt

Grated zest and juice of 2 to 3 organic lemons

Extra-virgin olive oil spray

Preheat the oven to 350°F to 400°F (180°C to 200°C). Line a baking sheet or pan with parchment paper.

Arrange the anchovies on the pan skin side down in a single layer. Sprinkle the cornmeal over the anchovies and press down gently to adhere. Sprinkle on the pine nuts, salt, lemon zest, and lemon juice.

Spray with olive oil and bake until browned on top, about 20 minutes.

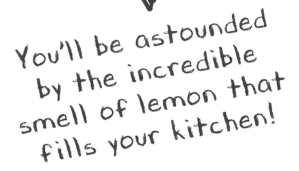

You'll be astounded by the incredible smell of lemon that fills your kitchen!

Pan de Mej

This recipe makes 6 large corn buns, but you can make them any size or shape that you like. I've even used this dough to make little tiny cookies.

✓ **MAKES 6 LARGE BUNS (ABOUT 4½ INCHES/11 CM IN DIAMETER)**

1¼ cups (200 g) finely ground cornmeal
¾ cup (100 g) rice flour or whole-grain durum flour
⅔ cup (80 g) organic powdered sugar
1½ teaspoons baking powder
Grated zest of 1 organic lemon
¼ cup (60 ml) organic corn oil
⅓ cup (75 ml) milk

Preheat the oven to 340°F (170°C). Line a baking sheet with parchment paper.

In a large bowl, combine the cornmeal, rice flour, sugar, baking powder, and lemon zest.

Stir the oil and milk into the dry ingredients and mix with a fork until combined. Divide the dough into 6 portions and form into buns, or use an ice cream scoop to make spheres.

Place the buns on the prepared pan and flatten them gently with your fingertips. Bake until the tops crack, about 20 minutes.

Variations

1 Add 1 teaspoon matcha green tea powder to the dough to give the buns a pleasant color and make them even better for you!

2 For a chocolate chip version, knead ⅔ cup (100 grams) chocolate chips into the dough and replace the dairy milk with almond milk.

#tasteandhealth

How I love GREEN TEA! Its benefits for your cardiovascular system (due to its high content of polyphenols, especially catechins) are well known, and its cancer-fighting abilities are still being studied. You should definitely always have green tea in your cupboard. (Obviously, I'm talking about tea leaves—not sweetened green tea-flavored beverages.) I especially love matcha, which is aromatic, herbaceous, and a beautiful green color. It's especially good for those with allergies, as it contains a catechin called epigallocatechin. Articles published in various international scientific journals suggest that this antioxidant blocks the histamine and immunoglobulin E involved in immune responses and typical allergy symptoms.

Green Toasts

You need an immersion blender and a mini food processor to prepare many of my recipes. Always have them at the ready.

✓ **SERVES 4**

Salt

1⅔ cups (250 g) shelled fresh or frozen peas

2½ ounces (70 g) goat cheese

5 fresh mint leaves

3 tablespoons plus 1 teaspoon (50 ml) extra-virgin olive oil

Pink peppercorns, to taste

Multigrain bread, sliced and toasted

In a saucepan of lightly salted water, cook the peas until just bright green, then drain and allow to cool.

Transfer the peas to a mini food processor. Add the goat cheese, mint leaves, oil, and pink peppercorns. With the machine running, add enough water (about 3 tablespoons/50 ml) in a thin stream to make a creamy spread.

Spread the pea mixture on the toasts.

Don't use canned peas. They won't give you the bright green color you want!

Falafel

I love falafel hot or cold. They even win over people who claim not to like beans dressed with olive oil and lemon juice!

✓ **SERVES 4**

Salt

⅔ cup (100 g) frozen shelled edamame

Leaves of 1 sprig parsley

1 yellow onion, peeled and cut into chunks

2 cups (500 g) canned chickpeas, drained and rinsed

5 tablespoons extra-virgin olive oil

Juice of 1 lemon

1 tablespoon ground cumin

½ teaspoon ground turmeric

3 tablespoons (30 g) finely ground cornmeal

Preheat the oven to 400°F (200°C). Line a baking pan with parchment paper.

In a saucepan of lightly salted water, blanch the edamame. Drain and let cool slightly.

In a food processor, combine the parsley and onion and process. Add the edamame, chickpeas, oil, lemon juice, cumin, and turmeric and process until the mixture forms a dense paste with a few chunkier chickpeas in it. Season to taste with salt.

Use a small ice cream scoop (or your hands) to form small balls of the mixture. Roll the balls in the cornmeal and set them on the prepared pan as you make them.

Bake until golden, at least 15 minutes.

P.S. You can also cook the falafel on the stovetop in a lightly but thoroughly oiled nonstick pan.

{ BASKET № 2 }

**Walnuts, Almonds,
Hazelnuts,
"Tipo 2" or White
Whole Wheat Flour,
Apples, Extra-Virgin Olive Oil,
Lentils, Raspberries**

RECIPES

Lentil and Walnut Salad _____ 55
Granola _____ 56
Kisses + Variation _____ 59
Apple-Walnut Salad with Balsamic-Honey
    Dressing _____ 60
Ricotta Berry Tartlets +
    Variations _____ 63
Pancakes with Bananas, Raspberries, and Honey ____ 64
Crumble + Variations _____ 67

#tasteandhealth

There is a great deal of scientific evidence showing that WALNUTS protect against chronic illnesses, including METABOLIC SYNDROME and TYPE 2 DIABETES. Eating walnuts also seems to improve body mass index (BMI) and body adiposity without causing weight gain: Participants in the PREDIMED study and in NHS and HPFS studies who ate large amounts of walnuts had lower body mass and smaller waist measurements. Like all nuts, walnuts do not contain cholesterol. Indeed, they can lower cholesterol if you make them a regular part of your diet!

Lentil and Walnut Salad

The trick to using herbs and spices is to keep them in a visible spot in your kitchen. We do the opposite with salt and keep very little at hand.

✓ **SERVES 4**

1½ cups (300 g) cooked lentils, well drained

1⅓ cups (150 g) walnuts, finely chopped

¾ cup (80 g) drained oil-packed sun-dried tomatoes, finely chopped

1 leek, white and light-green parts, minced

Leaves of 1 bunch parsley, minced

Finely grated zest and juice of 1 organic lemon

Extra-virgin olive oil

Piece of fresh ginger

In a large bowl, combine the cooked lentils, walnuts, sun-dried tomatoes, leek, and parsley and toss to combine well. Drizzle on the lemon juice, toss, and taste. Dress with a little olive oil if needed.

Sprinkle the lemon zest on top and grate a little ginger over the salad just before serving.

P.S. Sun-dried tomatoes are a source of concentrated iron, phosphorous, and, most of all, carotenoids. If you prefer not to use the type in oil, use dry-pack or salt-preserved dried tomatoes. You'll have to soak them in water for at least 30 minutes to soften. If they were salt-packed, rinse them very well to eliminate excess salt.

Granola

This is one of my most requested recipes and one that I love because it contains so many ingredients that are good for your health (especially thyroid health, thanks to all the iodine and selenium) in the proper amounts, and also because I see it as a way of being good to yourself starting with breakfast. I never go without breakfast: a cup of coffee, nice and bitter, yogurt, and granola!

✓ MAKES 5 TO 6 CUPS (600 TO 700 G)

5½ cups (500 g) rolled oats

½ cup (50 g) almonds, coarsely chopped

⅓ cup (50 g) hazelnuts, coarsely chopped

¼ cup (40 g) raisins, coarsely chopped

¾ cup (80 g) unsweetened shredded coconut

Pinch of salt

¼ cup (60 ml) organic corn oil

2 tablespoons plus 2 teaspoons (40 ml) organic sunflower oil

½ cup (130 ml) maple syrup

¼ cup plus 2 tablespoons (130 g) honey

Preheat the oven to 320°F (160°C). Line a baking sheet with parchment paper.

In a large bowl, combine the dry ingredients. Add the oils, maple syrup, and honey. Sprinkle on a couple of tablespoons of water and toss with your hands or a spatula until thoroughly combined. Spread on the prepared pan and bake for 20 minutes.

Remove the pan from the oven and mix the granola without breaking up any clumps. Bake until crunchy, an additional 10 to 20 minutes.

Remove from the oven and allow to cool. Use your hands to break up into irregular pieces.

Granola will keep for a couple of months in a tightly sealed glass container.

I never skip breakfast!

Kisses

As a kid I was curious about everything. I alternated between spending time with my mother, Cristina, in the kitchen—where she was often preparing these cookies—and spending time in my room, where I "studied" insects under a microscope.

MAKES 15 SANDWICH COOKIES

⅔ cup (100 g) blanched hazelnuts
1⅔ cups (200 g) white whole wheat flour or Italian "tipo 2" flour
⅔ cup (80 g) organic powdered sugar
¼ cup (60 ml) organic corn oil
⅔ cup (100 g) dark chocolate (72% cacao)

Preheat the oven to 350°F (180°C). Line a baking sheet with parchment paper and set aside.

In a mini food processor, grind the hazelnuts to a paste. The paste should feel oily.

In a bowl, combine the hazelnut paste, flour, sugar, and corn oil. Pull off a piece of the dough and with your hands shape it into a small ball. Place the ball on the prepared pan. Continue with remaining dough to make an even number of cookies. Flatten the balls slightly and bake until set and light golden, about 20 minutes.

Meanwhile, melt the chocolate in the top of a double boiler and cool until it has a thick consistency.

When the cookies have cooled, sandwich them in pairs with melted chocolate in between.

Variation

For friends with celiac disease: Replace the wheat flour with rice flour. Your cookies will be delicious!

Apple–Walnut Salad with Balsamic–Honey Dressing

Apples are packed with polyphenols, phytosterols, vitamin C, and pectin. Always keep a good supply on hand, and be sure to eat the peel (as long as it's organic, of course!).

SERVES 4

SALAD

2 heads Belgian endive, slivered
1 head radicchio, slivered
2 Granny Smith apples, peeled (if not organic) and diced
1¾ cups (200 g) walnuts, roughly chopped
⅓ cup (50 g) raisins

DRESSING

¼ cup (60 ml) extra-virgin olive oil
¼ cup plus 2 tablespoons (90 ml) balsamic vinegar
1 teaspoon honey
Pinch of salt

FOR THE SALAD: In a salad bowl, combine the Belgian endive, radicchio, apples, walnuts, and raisins.

FOR THE DRESSING: In a small bowl, whisk together the olive oil, balsamic, honey, and salt.

Drizzle the dressing over the salad and toss until well combined.

#tasteandhealth

A study published in the *Journal of the International Society of Sports Nutrition* demonstrated that young runners in the twenty to thirty age group have their best performances when they eat energy bars or raisins as supplements. RAISINS are energy in its purest form.

They are a good source of sugars and also contain fiber, calcium, and oleanolic acid (a powerful anti-inflammatory), in addition to potassium, calcium, and phosphorous. Thanks to their high content of phytonutrients, they are effective anti-inflammatories and antioxidants.

Ricotta Berry Tartlets

SERVES 6 TO 8

CRUST

2 cups (250 g) white whole wheat flour or Italian "tipo 2" flour

⅔ cup (80 g) organic powdered sugar

Finely grated zest of 1 organic lemon

¼ cup (60 ml) organic sunflower oil

FILLING

Generous 1 cup (250 g) Italian-style ricotta cheese or well-drained regular ricotta

½ cup (70 g) organic powdered sugar

⅓ cup (60 g) quartered strawberries

½ cup (60 g) raspberries

FOR THE CRUST: In a bowl, combine the flour, sugar, and lemon zest. Add the oil and ¼ cup (60 ml) water and knead together to form a smooth and compact dough. Shape the dough into a ball, wrap in plastic wrap, and refrigerate for 1 hour.

MEANWHILE, FOR THE FILLING: In a bowl, vigorously whisk the ricotta with the sugar until a cream-like density is reached.

Preheat the oven to 350°F (180°C).

Roll out the dough and cut out rounds to line disposable aluminum mini tartlet pans or silicone mini tartlet pans. (You can also roll the dough into a single large round and use it to line a 9-inch/23-cm tart pan.)

Put a few tablespoons of the ricotta filling in each tartlet shell and bake until light brown on top, 30 to 40 minutes. (The large tart will take about 10 minutes longer.) Cool the tart completely and top with the strawberries and raspberries.

Variations

These are so delicious! You can also vary them by folding about ¼ cup (50 g) diced candied fruit or about ½ cup (70 g) chocolate chips into the ricotta. Or fill the tartlets with ⅔ cup (200 g) of a healthy hazelnut spread and skip the ricotta completely. Top hazelnut tartlets with ¾ cup (70 grams) chopped hazelnuts.

Pancakes with Bananas, Raspberries, and Honey

Every night I set my alarm for 6:00 or 7:00 a.m. All night long I dream of recipes, and in the morning I jot them down as I'm making breakfast.

✓ **MAKES 12 PANCAKES**

1¾ cups plus 1 tablespoon (220 g) white whole wheat flour or Italian "tipo 2" flour

1½ cups (350 ml) milk

¼ cup (30 g) organic powdered sugar

½ teaspoon baking powder

1 tablespoon organic corn oil (for the pan)

2 bananas, sliced

1 pint (250 g) raspberries

2 tablespoons honey

In a large bowl, beat together the flour and milk, then beat in the sugar and baking powder. Be sure there are no lumps. (You can use an immersion blender if you like.)

Heat a nonstick pan over medium heat and add just a drop of oil. Pour about ¼ cup (60 ml) of the batter into the pan. When bubbles appear on the surface, flip the pancake and cook the other side. Repeat with the remaining batter and more oil.

Stack the pancakes, placing the banana slices, raspberries, and honey in between and on top of them.

Serve
them with
lots of fruit
and honey.

#tasteandhealth

No doubt about it: Hazelnuts are good for our DNA. Indeed, a recent study showed that regularly consuming HAZELNUTS can stabilize levels of LDL cholesterol—the "bad" kind—and triglycerides. And that's not all: They stop cellular aging and have anti-inflammatory and antiviral properties thanks to their selenium, vitamin E (the star antioxidant), and flavonoids.

Crumble

I started cooking with my daughter, Vivienne, when she was only fifteen months old. The first thing we made together was crumble—the best I've ever tasted!

Crumble is delicious with yogurt in the morning. You can also combine it with fresh fruit for a fantastic fruit crumble dessert: Cut fruits such as pears and apples into very small dice, spread in a pan, sprinkle the crumble on top, and bake. Or, if you prefer larger pieces of fruit, sauté them briefly before putting them in the pan.

√ **MAKES APPROXIMATELY 2½ CUPS (300 G) CRUMBLE**

¾ cup (120 g) blanched hazelnuts
1⅔ cups (200 g) white whole wheat flour or Italian "tipo 2" flour
¼ teaspoon baking powder
¼ cup plus 1 tablespoon (60 g) muscovado sugar
¼ cup (60 ml) organic sunflower oil
2 teaspoons honey

Preheat the oven to 340°F (170°C). Line a baking sheet with parchment paper.

Soak the hazelnuts in warm water for 50 minutes. Drain, but absolutely do not dry them! In a mini food processor, grind the nuts to coarse.

Transfer the hazelnuts to a bowl and stir in the flour, baking powder, sugar, oil, and honey.

Spread the mixture on the prepared pan. It should be in large, irregular pieces and not densely packed. Don't worry if it looks sandy.

Bake until crisp, about 20 minutes.

Variations

√ MAKES 2½ CUPS (300 G) CRUMBLE

Omit the wheat flour and use ¾ cup (100 g) brown rice flour and ½ cup plus 1 tablespoon (100 g) finely ground cornmeal.

1 **Do you have friends with celiac disease or are you interested in eating less gluten?**
Here's a gluten-free version!

2 **Interested in trying a cocoa crumble?**
Add a heaping tablespoon of sifted unsweetened cocoa powder.

{ BASKET Nº 3 }

**Chickpea Flour,
"Tipo 2" or White
Whole Wheat Flour,
Leeks, Pumpkin,
Extra-Virgin Olive Oil,
Frozen Peas**

RECIPES

Savory Leek Tart + Variation _____ 70
Eggless Leek Frittata _____ 73
Pumpkin Soup with Ginger + Variation _____ 74
Pumpkin and Chickpea Spread _____ 77
Pea, Zucchini, and Goat Cheese Pesto + Variation __ 78
Greek Chickpea and Zucchini
    "Meatballs" + Variations _____ 81
Mediterranean Sushi _____ 82

Savory Leek Tart

This is the perfect appetizer. Slice it into wedges and serve it right on a cutting board as the first course for a dinner with friends. It can be made in advance, too. In fact, it tastes even better if it has a chance to sit!

√ SERVES 6

CRUST

2⅔ cups (300 g) white whole wheat flour or Italian "tipo 2" flour
Pinch of salt
Pinch of baking soda
⅓ cup (80 ml) extra-virgin olive oil
2 tablespoons apple cider vinegar

FILLING

Extra-virgin olive oil, for sautéing
4 leeks, thinly sliced
Salt and pepper
Generous 1 cup (250 g) Italian-style ricotta cheese or well-drained regular ricotta

FOR THE CRUST: In a bowl, combine the flour, salt, baking soda, oil, and vinegar and knead by hand, adding water a tablespoon or so at a time, until you have a smooth and compact dough. (You will need about ½ cup/120 ml water.) Shape into a ball, wrap in plastic wrap, and refrigerate for 1 hour.

MEANWHILE, FOR THE FILLING: In a nonstick skillet, heat a few tablespoons olive oil over medium-high heat. Add the leeks, season with a pinch of salt and pepper, and cook until softened. When the leeks are soft, add the ricotta. Stir until well combined, then remove from the heat.

Preheat the oven to 350°F (180°C). Line the bottom of a 6-inch (15-cm) pie pan or earthenware dish with a round of parchment paper.

Roll out the crust and use it to line the prepared pan. Fill the crust with the ricotta filling and bake until the crust is well done, 45 to 50 minutes.

Variation

Replace the leeks and ricotta with 2 cups (400 g) diced peeled pumpkin or winter squash, 5 ounces (150 g) soft goat cheese, and fresh thyme leaves.

Cook the pumpkin in a nonstick pan with a drizzle of oil, a spoonful or two of water, and a little salt and pepper. When the squash is soft, blend with the goat cheese and thyme. Make and fill the tart shell as above and bake at 350°F (180°C) until the crust is well done, 45 to 50 minutes.

With leeks

With pumpkin

Eggless Leek Frittata

My daughter, Vivienne, goes crazy for this dish. Her personal preference is the addition of a little fresh rosemary (picked by her) at the end and some grated aged sheep's cheese in place of the salt. She's a real gourmet! Obviously, you can customize it any way you like.

SERVES 4 TO 6

2 cups plus 3 tablespoons (200 g) chickpea flour
1⅔ cups (400 ml) lukewarm water
¼ teaspoon salt
Pinch of pepper
Extra-virgin olive oil
2 leeks, thinly sliced

In a large bowl, whisk together the chickpea flour and water by hand or using an immersion blender until thoroughly blended. There should not be any lumps.

Stir in the salt and pepper and a couple of tablespoons of extra-virgin olive oil. Stir again and let the batter rest in the refrigerator for 20 minutes.

Stir the leeks into the batter.

Lightly oil a nonstick skillet with olive oil and place over medium-high heat until the pan is very hot. Pour enough batter into the pan to fill the whole pan but be no deeper than ¼ inch (0.5 cm). Cook for about 10 minutes, then flip the frittata out onto a plate. Return it to the pan browned side up and cook the second side for another 10 minutes. Continue with more batter and oil (how many frittatas you can make will depend on the size of your pan).

P.S. You can also bake the frittata. Preheat the oven to 425°F (220°C). Line an 8-inch (20-cm) baking pan with parchment paper. Pour in the batter and bake until set and nicely browned, about 20 minutes. Brush the surface of the pan lightly with oil. There's no need to flip the frittata if you bake it. Once it is cooked, cut into squares and serve warm!

Pumpkin Soup with Ginger

Pumpkin has been used for its calming effects since ancient times. It also assists in the production of serotonin and is rich in beta-carotene, which protects us from free radicals and is a good anti-inflammatory.

SERVES 4

3 tablespoons extra-virgin olive oil

1 winter squash (2½ lbs/1.2 kg), such as pumpkin, kabocha, or kuri, peeled, seeded, and diced

1 shallot, minced

1¼ cups (300 ml) milk

Salt and pepper

1 piece ginger, peeled, grated to taste

¾ cup (200 g) canned cannellini, drained and rinsed

In a Dutch oven or soup pot, heat the oil over medium heat. Add the squash, shallot, and a few tablespoons of water and cook the squash to soften. When the squash is about halfway cooked, add the milk and season with salt and pepper. Grate in the ginger, stir to combine, and continue cooking until the squash is soft.

Add the beans and ½ cup (120 ml) water, then use an immersion blender to puree until smooth. Your soup is ready.

Variation

To make this into a one-pot meal, add 3 potatoes (sweet potatoes work well) or 1⅔ cups (320 g) black rice, brown basmati rice, or barley, along with 2¼ cups (500 ml) milk, or simply serve with a few slices of toasted whole-grain bread.

#tasteandhealth

GINGER is a plant in the same family as cardamom and hails from the Far East. It contains various healthful substances—zingiberene and gingerols—that are strong anti-inflammatories and anti-oxidants that fight cancer. It also aids digestion and has a positive effect on the gastro-intestinal system. It is often used to calm the nausea of motion sickness and morning sickness, as well as alleviate indigestion and flatulence. Fresh ginger may be grated, or you can crush it using a garlic press (though do set one aside just for this purpose). Dried ginger (the kind without sugar) is excellent! When I begin to lose my voice, I find it the best remedy. I eat a little cube every 2 hours during the day, and by evening I'm back to normal!

Pumpkin and Chickpea Spread

Use every part of the pumpkin! Save the seeds and eat them raw or roast them. Not only do they make a tasty snack, but they're rich in cucurbitin, which is a big help with many urinary issues in both men and women. Serve with crackers or crudites.

SERVES 4

2¾ cups (14 oz/400 g) diced, peeled, and seeded winter squash, such as pumpkin, kabocha, or kuri

Extra-virgin olive oil

⅔ cup (150 g) canned chickpeas, drained and rinsed

⅔ cup (100 g) feta cheese

Fresh thyme leaves

In a nonstick skillet, braise the squash in a small amount of olive oil with a few tablespoons of water over medium heat until softened.

Transfer the squash to a blender and add the chickpeas and feta. Puree to spreading consistency.

Transfer the mixture to a bowl, brush the surface of the spread with olive oil and sprinkle with the fresh thyme. Cover and refrigerate for 1 hour to firm up.

Pea, Zucchini, and Goat Cheese Pesto

This is the perfect condiment to elevate any dish and make it unique! Use this pesto on pasta or barley, or spread it on toasted whole wheat bread! If you prepare the pesto in advance, oil the surface so it won't turn brown and will maintain its great taste!

MAKES ABOUT 2 CUPS (500 G)

3 zucchini, sliced into rounds
1 cup (150 g) frozen peas
1 shallot, diced
¼ cup (60 ml) extra-virgin olive oil
3 ounces (80 g) goat cheese
Salt and pepper

In a large skillet, cook the zucchini slices, peas, and shallot in a small amount of water until tender. When they are about halfway done, add the olive oil and continue cooking.

Transfer the mixture to a blender, add the goat cheese and a pinch of salt and pepper, and puree.

Variation

MAKES ABOUT 2 CUPS (500 G)

1⅓ cups (200 g) frozen peas
2⅔ cups (400 g) frozen shelled edamame
1 yellow onion, thinly sliced
Salt and pepper
3 tablespoons extra-virgin olive oil
Scant ½ cup (100 g) Italian-style ricotta cheese or well-drained regular ricotta

Edamame, Pea, and Ricotta Pesto
In a skillet, cook the peas, edamame, and onion in a few tablespoons of water with a pinch of salt and pepper. When they are about halfway done, add the olive oil and continue cooking.

Transfer half of the cooked pea mixture to a blender. Add the ricotta and puree. Your pesto is ready! Use this pesto on pasta, ravioli, barley, farro—anything you like, really. Serve the dish garnished with the remaining whole peas and edamame and a generous grinding of black pepper.

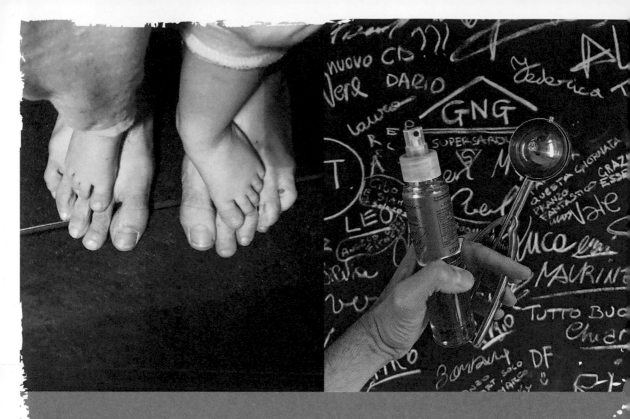

#tasteandhealth

LEGUMES contain as much protein as meat and twice as much as grains. They also contain four essential amino acids (lysine, threonine, valine, and tryptophan) and, when combined with grains, meet our daily requirements for those substances.

According to a study published in the *American Journal of Clinical Nutrition*, eating a serving of about ¾ cup (130 g) of beans per day can help with weight loss. Participants in the study lost ¾ pound (0.34 kg) over six weeks without changing their diets, simply by adding a serving of legumes each day. That change also led to a 31 percent increase in feeling full and satisfied.

Greek Chickpea and Zucchini "Meatballs"

A spray bottle of oil and at least two ice cream scoops of varying sizes are musts for the kitchen. Use them to make excellent vegetarian "meatballs" that can be baked or cooked on the stovetop until crisp but not greasy!

SERVES 4

2 zucchini
5 tablespoons extra-virgin olive oil
10 fresh mint leaves, minced
Salt and pepper
¼ cup (40 g) chickpea flour

Preheat the oven to 350°F (180°C). Line a baking sheet with parchment paper.

Grate the zucchini on the largest holes of a box grater into a bowl.

Add the oil and mint to the zucchini and season with salt and pepper. Add the chickpea flour and mix until well combined.

Using a standard ice cream scoop (or your hands), form the mixture into balls and place them on the prepared pan.

Spray the balls with a small amount of olive oil and bake until firm and lightly browned, about 20 minutes.

Variations

1 Replace the zucchini with two standard-size sweet potatoes. So good!

2 You can also use an equal amount by weight of two standard-size finely grated carrots in place of the grated zucchini. Bake for same amount of time as above.

81

Mediterranean Sushi

I call this Mediterranean sushi, though it's really a whole wheat flat bread wrapped around an eggless frittata. If there's anything in the ingredient list you don't like, feel free to leave it out—except for the chickpea flour, of course! But if you don't make this you're really missing out!

✓ **SERVES 4**

2 cups plus 3 tablespoons (200 g) chickpea flour

1⅔ cups (400 ml) lukewarm water

¼ teaspoon salt

8 oil-packed sun-dried tomatoes (50 g), minced

½ teaspoon curry powder

Extra-virgin olive oil

Three 8-inch (20-cm) round whole wheat flatbreads (such as piedina, naan, or flour tortillas), preferably made with extra-virgin olive oil

About 1 cup (200 g) spreadable cheese

In a large bowl, beat the chickpea flour and water with a whisk or immersion blender until smooth. There should be no lumps.

Stir in the salt, sun-dried tomatoes, curry powder, and a couple of tablespoons of olive oil. Stir again to combine, then refrigerate for about 30 minutes.

Lightly oil an 8-inch (20-cm) nonstick skillet and heat over medium-high heat until very hot. Add enough batter to cover the bottom of the pan and come a scant ⅛ inch (a few millimeters) up the sides of the pan. Cook for 10 minutes, flip and return to the pan, then cook on the second side for 10 minutes. Repeat to make 3 of these eggless frittatas and allow them to cool.

Gently reheat the flatbreads on the stovetop (the same pan you used is fine) and spread a spoonful of cheese on each. Arrange an eggless frittata on top of the cheese. Roll up and cut into spirals.

P.S. These Mediterranean sushi rolls are good cold, but you can also reheat them on the stovetop before serving if you prefer.

Fill with seasonal herbs!

{ BASKET Nº 4 }

**Beets,
Chickpeas, Avocado,
Celery, Feta Cheese,
Apple, Ginger**

RECIPES

Beet Chips _____ 86
Beet Cake _____ 87
Hummus + Variation _____ 88
Chickpea, Celery, and Feta Salad + Variations _____ 91
Avocado Tartare with Lime and Red Onion _____ 92
Celery, Apple, and Ginger Juice + Alternative _____ 95

Beet Chips

Beets are an excellent source of iron. Beet chips are sweet—kids love them. Try them and you'll see!

✓ **SERVES 4**

3 beets
Extra-virgin olive oil spray
Salt and pepper

Preheat the oven to 425°F (220°C). Line a baking sheet with parchment paper.

Use a mandoline to very thinly slice the beets. Arrange them on the prepared pan. Spray with olive oil and season with salt and pepper

Bake until crispy and purple, about 40 minutes.

P.S. Beets stain everything, and I mean everything—cutting boards, hands, and even urine, so don't panic if your children pee red after chowing down on these chips!

Beet Cake

This cake is excellent for athletes in training. It combines betaine from beets with the polyphenol and antioxidant activity of cocoa powder and helps to increase muscle strength.

✓ MAKES ONE 9-INCH (23-CM) CAKE/8 TO 10 SERVINGS

4 ounces (120 g) cooked beets, store-bought or homemade

¾ cup (180 ml) unsweetened almond milk

1 cup (150 g) almonds, roughly chopped

1 cup (130 g) all-purpose flour

⅔ cup (70 g) whole wheat flour

¼ cup plus 2 tablespoons (80 g) muscovado sugar

1 teaspoon unsweetened cocoa powder

1 tablespoon baking powder

Scant ⅓ cup (70 ml) organic corn oil

3½ ounces (100 g) dark chocolate (72% cacao), cut up

Preheat the oven to 350°F (180°C). Line the bottom of a 9-inch (23-cm) cake pan with a round of parchment paper.

In a mini food processor, puree the cooked beets with about half of the almond milk.

In a bowl, mix together the almonds, flours, sugar, cocoa powder, and baking powder. Add the pureed beet mixture to the dry ingredients along with the corn oil and stir to combine.

Place the chocolate and the remaining almond milk in the top of a double boiler and melt, whisking together. Stir into the batter.

Pour the batter into the prepared pan. Bake until a toothpick inserted in the center comes out clean, about 50 minutes. If the toothpick comes out with some batter clinging to it, the cake still needs to bake a little longer.

Hummus

I make hummus at least twice a week to spread on bread or toasts, or as a dip for seasonal vegetables.

✓ **MAKES ABOUT 2 CUPS (500 G)**

2 cups (500 g) canned chickpeas, drained and rinsed
2 tablespoons tahini
½ clove garlic
Pinch of ground cumin
Pinch of sweet paprika
¼ cup (60 ml) extra-virgin olive oil
Juice of 1 lemon

In a food processor, puree all the ingredients until smooth. (Omit the garlic if raw garlic is hard for you to digest.) The resulting creamy spread can be served with raw vegetables, toasted bread, focaccia—anything you like. You can even eat it with a spoon!

Variation

To make beet hummus, use ½ Tropea red onion (Italian torpedo onion) in place of the garlic and add 7 ounces (200 g) cooked beets (about two small beets). Puree all the ingredients together, adding a tablespoon or two of water, if necessary, to make a creamy mixture.

Beet Hummus   Classic Hummus

#tasteandhealth

CHICKPEAS are one of my favorite legumes. I love them in everything. They're rich in magnesium and folate and reduce homocysteine—high levels of this amino acid in the blood increase the risk of heart attack and stroke.

That's not the only heart-health benefit of eating chickpeas: They also lower LDL ("bad") cholesterol and contain lots of omega-3s, which means they prevent depression and lower triglycerides, which in turn fosters a regular heartbeat and decreases the chance of arrhythmia.

Chickpea, Celery, and Feta Salad

Celery is the cook's best friend. You can use every part of it, and it's a good low-calorie snack that has lots of potassium.

✓ **SERVES 4**

2 cups (500 g) canned chickpeas, drained and rinsed
1 cup (150 g) diced feta cheese
1 stalk celery, finely diced
Extra-virgin olive oil
Juice of 1 lemon

In a bowl, combine the chickpeas, feta, and celery. Dress with a drizzle of olive oil and the lemon juice.

P.S. Don't strip the leaves from your celery and toss them! Chop the leaves and serve them like lettuce in a salad: they contain vitamin C, chlorophyll, and lots of key minerals.

Variations

1 In place of the feta use a soft, spreadable cow's milk cheese, such as Quartirolo Lombardo cheese, or an aged sheep's milk cheese.

2 For a vegan salad, use smoked tofu in place of the cheese.

Avocado Tartare with Lime and Red Onion

Avocado is a source of good fats that protect the cardiovascular system. The Italian avocados from Sicily are excellent—give them a try!

SERVES 4

2 avocados, finely diced
1 small red onion, minced
Juice of 1 lime
Salt and pepper
Extra-virgin olive oil

In a bowl, combine the avocados and onion. Drizzle the lime juice over the avocado and onion. Season with salt and pepper and drizzle on a little olive oil.

Use a ring mold to arrange the tartare on plates.

If you don't have a ring mold, you can serve the tartare in a bowl or use it to top toasted bread for a special bruschetta.

You can serve it on bruschetta!

Beet, apple, and ginger

Celery, apple, and ginger

Celery, Apple, and Ginger Juice

This juice and the alternative below are anti-inflammatory and help you digest. They are also very rich in minerals. One thing I would like to note: pineapple does not "melt fat," as is often said, but instead aids in the digestion of protein.

✓ SERVES 4

½ piece (3 g) fresh ginger, peeled
2 Granny Smith apples, cut into chunks
2 stalks celery, cut into chunks
¼ pineapple, peeled and cut into chunks

Scrub the apples and celery. Combine all the ingredients in a juicer. Taste the results!

P.S. Celery leaves are full of chlorophyll, so don't throw them away! Don't throw away the pineapple core either, because that is the most concentrated source of its nutrients and is perfect for using in juices!

Alternative

✓ SERVES 4

1 raw beet, peeled and cut into chunks
2 Granny Smith apples, cut into chunks
¼ piece (2 g) fresh ginger, peeled
1 grapefruit, peeled, pulled into sections

Beet, Apple, and Ginger Juice
Combine all the ingredients in a juicer. Taste the results!

You can use a lemon or a lime in place of the grapefruit if you prefer.

{ BASKET Nº 5 }

Coconut, Carrots, Chocolate, Eggplant, Fresh Mint

RECIPES

Carrot-Yogurt Shots + Variation _____ 98

Chocolate Roll _____ 101

Individual Chocolate Lava Cakes + Variations _____ 102

Coconut Treats + Variations _____ 104

Carrot Muffins + Variation _____ 107

Pasta with Eggplant, Taggiasca Olives,
Capers, and Mint _____ 108

Matcha Crêpes _____ 110

Carrot-Yogurt Shots

Gathering together is an important part of cooking. Cooking with friends and eating all together is one of the best parts of life! It's the foundation of the food pyramid.

✓ **SERVES 6 TO 8**

11 ounces (300 g) carrots
 (4 to 6 medium), sliced
½ cup (80 g) blanched almonds
½ cup (120 g) nonfat Greek yogurt
Extra-virgin olive oil
Salt
Fresh thyme leaves

In a saucepan, combine the carrots with water to cover and bring to a boil. Cook the carrots until soft, then drain.

Transfer the carrots to a food processor and add the almonds. Process, adding as much water as necessary to make a creamy smooth puree.

In a bowl, whisk the yogurt with a little oil and a pinch of salt.

Put a spoonful of the yogurt mixture into the bottom of each of 6 to 8 liqueur glasses or small jars. Top with the carrot puree. Garnish with a few thyme leaves.

P.S. Add a few crumbled saffron threads to the yogurt for an even more colorful treat.

Variation

For a vegan version, omit the yogurt. Puree 4 ounces (120 g) soft tofu with some oil, salt, and thyme. Layer with the carrot-almond mixture as directed.

Carrots and almonds

Yogurt

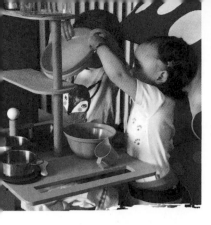

Chocolate Roll

This dessert is great year-round. I always have it in my favorite storage area—my freezer. You can customize it any way you like. Make it and cut it into cubes. You'll find you keep reaching for another piece, and another, and another . . .

SERVES 8 TO 10

- 1 pound 5 ounces (600 g) dark chocolate (72% cacao)
- 1 espresso cup (3 to 4 tablespoons) brewed espresso
- 1¼ cups (300 ml) soy milk or almond milk
- 2 tablespoons organic corn oil
- 1 pound (500 g) whole wheat digestive biscuits or graham crackers
- ⅓ cup (50 g) blanched hazelnuts

Place the chocolate, espresso, and milk in the top of a double boiler. Melt the chocolate and whisk to combine. Stir in the oil. Crumble the cookies and stir them in as well. Fold in the hazelnuts (left whole).

Transfer the mixture to a silicone loaf pan and freeze for 5 hours until very firm.

Once the roll is firm, it is ready to serve.

Unmold. (It will come out of the silicone mold easily.) Cut into slices and then into cubes!

You can use other nuts in place of the hazelnuts, or fold in chopped dried apricots, prunes, dried figs, or any other dried fruit.

Individual Chocolate Lava Cakes

Making individual cakes means each diner gets to cut into one and see the chocolate flow. But they are also good cold: The centers will thicken up a little and won't be as runny, but they'll still be soft.

✓ **MAKES 6 TO 8 CAKES**

7 ounces (200 g) dark chocolate (72% cacao), cut into chunks

½ cup plus 3 tablespoons (200 ml) soy milk or almond milk

2 tablespoons organic corn oil

⅓ cup (30 g) unsweetened cocoa powder

¼ cup plus 1 tablespoon (60 g) muscovado sugar

⅔ cup (80 g) white whole wheat flour or Italian "tipo 2" flour

2 teaspoons baking powder

Pinch of salt

Preheat the oven to 350°F (180°C).

Melt the chocolate with the milk in a double boiler. Whisk together, then add the oil, cocoa powder, sugar, flour, baking powder, and salt and whisk vigorously to combine, whisking in as much air as possible.

Divide the batter among six to eight 2.5-inch (7-cm) ramekins. Transfer the ramekins to a baking sheet and bake 12 to 13 minutes.

Variations

✓ **INGREDIENTS FOR COFFEE-FLAVORED CAKES**

7 ounces (200 g) dark chocolate (72% cacao), cut into chunks

½ cup plus 3 tablespoons (200 ml) soy milk or almond milk

1 espresso cup (3 to 4 tablespoons) brewed coffee

⅓ cup (30 g) unsweetened cocoa powder

2 tablespoons very finely ground coffee

¼ cup plus 1 tablespoon (60 g) muscovado sugar

3 tablespoons (40 ml) organic corn oil

⅓ cup (80 g) white whole wheat or Italian "tipo 2" flour

2 teaspoons baking powder

Pinch of salt

1 Coffee-Flavored Lava Cakes

Preheat the oven to 350°F (180°C). Melt the chocolate with the milk in a double boiler and whisk together. Add the remaining ingredients and whisk vigorously to combine, whisking in as much air as possible. Divide the batter among the ramekins and bake as directed above.

2 Coconut-Flavored Lava Cakes

For a coconut version, incorporate 1 scant cup (100 g) coconut flour in place of the wheat flour.

#tasteandhealth

Everyone who follows me knows that I could eat chocolate all day long, as long as it's DARK CHOCOLATE (at least 72 percent cacao!). There is a great deal of scientific literature on chocolate's benefits. Indeed, according to many studies, the FLAVONOIDS in cacao have beneficial effects on blood pressure and cholesterol and also decrease headaches and fight stress. A recent study at Brown University (in Providence, Rhode Island) associated consumption of cacao with prevention of diabetes and heart disease.

Clearly dark chocolate is A HEALTHY ADDITION TO YOUR DIET. It's a mood enhancer and stimulates the creation of serotonin, which means it makes you feel relaxed and happy. It also contains a lot of nutrients, such as copper, iron, zinc, and a good dose of magnesium (520 mg in 100 g of chocolate). If you pair it with unsweetened coffee, its anti-inflammatory powers increase considerably!!!

Coconut Treats

These are quick and easy. When I make them with Vivienne, the batter mysteriously tends to disappear before I can get them in the oven. That's why I work quickly using an ice cream scoop!

✓ **MAKES 20 COOKIES**

- 2 cups (200 g) unsweetened shredded coconut
- 1¼ cups plus 3 tablespoons (170 g) white whole wheat flour or Italian "tipo 2" flour
- ½ cup (70 g) organic powdered sugar
- 1½ teaspoons baking powder
- 1 cup plus 1 tablespoon (250 ml) milk
- 3 tablespoons light-flavored extra-virgin olive oil or organic sunflower oil

Preheat the oven to 325°F (160°C). Line a baking sheet with parchment paper.

In a bowl, stir together the coconut, flour, sugar, baking powder, milk, and oil. Use a standard ice cream scoop to make small balls of dough and place them on the prepared baking sheet.

Bake until lightly browned, 17 to 20 minutes.

Coconut, Carrot, and Chocolate Treats never last long!

Variations

1 Add 1 cup (50 g) grated carrots and ¼ teaspoon ground turmeric to the dough.

2 Add a generous ½ cup (80 g) chocolate chips and replace the dairy milk with soy milk.

Carrot Muffins

Desserts made with carrots are tricky because carrots contain a lot of water that is released as they bake. These muffins are exceptional tasting and they come out beautifully every time, as long as you follow the recipe exactly!

✓ **MAKES 12 MUFFINS**

MUFFINS

¾ cup plus 1 tablespoon (100 g) whole wheat flour
1 cup (130 g) semolina flour
¼ cup (50 g) muscovado sugar
2 teaspoons baking powder
Generous pinch of ground cinnamon
Generous 1 cup (250 g) nonfat dairy yogurt or nondairy yogurt, or generous ¾ cup (250 g) 0% Greek yogurt
5 tablespoons mild-flavored extra-virgin olive oil or organic sunflower oil
3 tablespoons maple syrup or honey
5 cups (250 g) grated carrots (about 10 medium)
½ cup (100 g) chopped hazelnuts

GLAZE (OPTIONAL)

6 tablespoons organic powdered sugar
Pinch of pepper

Preheat the oven to 350°F (180°C). Line the cups of a 12-cup muffin tin with paper liners.

FOR THE MUFFINS: In a large bowl, stir together the flour, semolina, sugar, baking powder, cinnamon, yogurt, oil, and maple syrup. Fold in the carrots and hazelnuts.

Divide the batter among the muffin cups and bake until lightly browned, about 25 minutes. Let the muffins cool.

IF DESIRED, FOR THE GLAZE: In a small bowl, combine the powdered sugar and 2 tablespoons water.

Dip each muffin upside down in the glaze, then turn right side up and allow the glaze to dry. Sprinkle with a pinch of pepper just before serving!

Variation

For gluten-free muffins, simply replace the whole wheat flour and the semolina flour with ¾ cup (100 g) rice flour and ¼ cup (50 g) potato starch.

Pasta with Eggplant, Taggiasca Olives, Capers, and Mint

This dish takes me back to a vacation in Greece and a fantastic pastitsio I enjoyed there that used these ingredients—a delicious memory.

SERVES 4

Salt

12 ounces (320 g) short-cut whole wheat pasta

¼ cup (60 ml) extra-virgin olive oil, plus additional for drizzling

1 pound (450 g) eggplant (about 1 medium)

⅔ cup (80 g) pitted Taggiasca or Niçoise olives

¼ cup plus 2 tablespoons (50 g) capers, rinsed and drained

5 tablespoons tomato paste

10 fresh mint leaves, minced

In a large pot of lightly salted boiling water, cook the pasta, stirring frequently, until al dente. Drain, rinse under running water, and transfer to a large bowl. Drizzle with a little olive oil and set aside.

Dice the eggplant and place it in a dry nonstick skillet. Cook over medium heat, stirring constantly, until it releases its natural liquids. When the eggplant is soft, add the ¼ cup olive oil, olives, capers, and tomato paste. Cook for about 10 minutes.

Toss together the pasta, eggplant mixture, and mint.

Try it warm!

P.S. This dish is meant to be served at room temperature, but I can attest that it is also delicious served slightly warm with aged ricotta cheese grated over the top just before serving.

#tasteandhealth

TOMATOES get their red hue from lycopene, a carotenoid that is an antioxidant and fights cancer and aging. Our bodies don't synthesize lycopene, so it has to be introduced through diet.

Tomato paste and cooked ripe tomatoes have higher lycopene content than raw tomatoes. That's because heat releases lycopene from inside the cells of the tomato and makes it easier for the digestive system to absorb.

Matcha Crêpes

Matcha is a highly prized green tea packed with polyphenols. To make matcha, green tea leaves are dried and then ground into a powder.

✓ **MAKES ABOUT 6 CRÊPES**

⅔ cup (70 g) whole-grain farro flour

¼ cup (30 g) organic powdered sugar

1 teaspoon matcha powder

¾ cup (170 ml) soy milk

2 tablespoons organic corn oil

4 ounces (120 g) dark chocolate (85% cacao), shaved

In a bowl, combine the flour, sugar, and matcha powder. Beat in the soy milk and corn oil.

Heat an 8-inch (20-cm) nonstick pan over medium heat. Add just enough batter to cover the bottom of the pan (about 3 tablespoons), tilting the pan so it goes to all the edges. Cook on the first side for a few minutes until set and lightly browned on the bottom, then carefully flip and cook the second side.

Transfer the crepe to a plate and scatter the chocolate over the crêpe while it's still hot so it will melt. Fold and serve.

Continue to make more crepes in the same manner.

P.S. You can find matcha powder in organic food stores, herbal shops, and grocery stores specializing in ethnic and Asian foods.

{ BASKET № 6 }

"Tipo 2" or White Whole Wheat Flour, Spices, Cannellini, Cabbage, Ginger

RECIPES

Cannellini and Tuna "Meatballs" + Variations ——— 115
Gingerbread Men ——— 116
Barley Risotto-Style with Pepper and
    Goat Cheese Cream + Variation ——— 119
Mini Focaccia Breads with Seeds and Olives ——— 121
Stuffed Cabbage with Cannellini Puree ——— 122
Pan dei Morti Cookies ——— 125

Cannellini and Tuna "Meatballs"

Frying strictly forbidden? Absolutely not, as long as it's done properly in a generous amount of peanut or extra-virgin olive oil, though you should still only indulge in peanut oil once or twice a month. If we want to eat something crispy more often, I use the oven and a good oil sprayed from a bottle!

✓ **SERVES 4**

2 cups (500 g) canned cannellini, drained and rinsed
1 can (3 oz/100 g) water-packed tuna, drained
1 shallot, peeled and cut into chunks
Leaves of 1 bunch parsley
1¾ cups (200 g) dried whole wheat breadcrumbs
Salt
Extra-virgin olive oil, plus olive oil spray

Preheat the oven to 400°F (200°C). Line a baking sheet with parchment paper.

In a food processor, pulse together the beans, tuna, shallot, and parsley. Don't puree the mixture too smooth. You want a fairly chunky mixture. If it seems too wet to hold together, add ½ to ⅔ cup (50 to 80 g) breadcrumbs.

Season with salt and drizzle with olive oil.

Spread the remaining breadcrumbs on a large dinner plate or sheet pan. Use a standard ice cream scoop to form "meatballs" of the bean mixture, dredge them in the breadcrumbs, and transfer to the prepared pan.

Spray the surface of the "meatballs" with olive oil and bake until lightly browned, about 20 minutes.

Variations

Prefer not to use tuna? Replace it with ⅔ cup (60 g) grated cheese or 3 ounces (80 g) tofu.

Gingerbread Men

Christmas wouldn't be Christmas without gingerbread men. Serve them with hot chocolate, give them to friends as gifts, and use them to decorate your tree!

✓ MAKES 6 TO 8 COOKIES

2 cups (250 g) white whole wheat flour or Italian "tipo 2" flour
¼ cup plus 1 tablespoon (60 g) muscovado sugar
1 teaspoon baking soda (or alternately 3 teaspoons baking powder)
1 teaspoon ground ginger
1 teaspoon ground cinnamon
1 teaspoon grated nutmeg
Pinch of salt
1 tablespoon honey
¼ cup (60 ml) organic corn oil
Scant ⅓ cup (70 ml) soy milk

Preheat the oven to 325° to 350°F (160° to 170°C). Line a baking sheet with parchment paper.

In a large bowl, combine the flour, sugar, baking soda, spices, and salt. Add the honey, corn oil, and soy milk (a little at a time) and stir to combine. The mixture should form a dough that can be kneaded by hand.

On a lightly floured surface, roll out the dough to about 1 inch (a few millimeters) thick and cut out cookies using the classic gingerbread man cutter. Gather the scraps and re-roll to cut out more cookies.

Transfer to the prepared pan and bake until lightly browned, about 10 minutes.

The perfect Christmas gift!

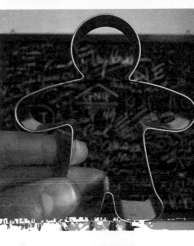

Fresh thyme leaves make this dish smell incredible!

Barley Risotto-Style with Pepper and Goat Cheese Cream

I love barley, oats, and farro cooked risotto-style, in soups, and in cold and warm salads. This is one of my favorite recipes! It combines peppers with barley for a delicious, healthful dish that will also keep your cholesterol in check!

✓ SERVES 4

Salt

1⅔ cups (320 g) pearled barley

2 medium red bell peppers (about 5 oz/150 g each), cut into thin strips

1 spring onion, sliced

Fresh thyme leaves

Extra-virgin olive oil

7 ounces (200 g) goat cheese

2 tablespoons (20 g) capers, drained

¼ cup (40 g) pine nuts, toasted

In a saucepan, bring 3⅓ cups (790 ml) lightly salted water to a boil. Add the barley and cook until the grains have completely absorbed the liquid.

Meanwhile, in a skillet, cook the peppers, spring onion, and thyme to taste with a little water and a little oil. When the vegetables are soft, transfer them to a blender and puree with the goat cheese. With the machine running, drizzle in a little olive oil.

Transfer a couple of spoonfuls of the cooked barley to a mini food processor and puree with a couple of spoonfuls of warm water. Return the barley puree to the pan of whole cooked barley and stir in the pepper and goat cheese cream. Cook over medium heat for 5 minutes to combine the ingredients.

Serve garnished with more thyme, capers, and pine nuts dotted here and there.

Variation

For a delicious twist, replace the goat cheese with the same amount of Greek yogurt. Garnish with a few sun-dried tomatoes.

#tasteandhealth

PEPPERS are one of summer's culinary superstars. They're used fresh in all kinds of sauces, and we also like to put them up in jars so we can eat them in the fall and winter as well. Peppers are full of phosphorous and potassium, as well as vitamins: they contain more VITAMIN C than any other vegetable! In 4 ounces (100 g) of peppers there are 153 mg. (The same amount of oranges contains only 50 mg.) Peppers are also rich in flavonoids, which strengthen the cardiovascular system by making blood vessels more elastic and protect against prostate disease.

Mini Focaccia Breads with Seeds and Olives

These make a healthy appetizer and a delicious savory snack. Homemade focaccia is good for you and tastes great!

✓ MAKES 8 TO 10 MINI FOCACCIA

1 envelope (2¼ teaspoons) active dry yeast or ⅓ cake (about 8 g) compressed fresh yeast

½ cup plus 1 tablespoon (135 ml) milk, warm

1½ cups (190 g) all-purpose flour

½ cup (60 g) whole wheat flour

Pinch of salt

2 tablespoons extra-virgin olive oil

½ cup (60 g) pitted whole Taggiasca or Niçoise olives

½ cup (70 g) sunflower, poppy, fennel, or other seeds

In a small bowl, dissolve the yeast in the milk. Place the flours and salt in a large bowl and make a well in the center. Add the milk mixture and mix to form a dough, kneading until well combined. Knead in the oil. If the dough feels very dry, add water, about a tablespoon at a time, until you have a soft, smooth dough. Knead the dough briskly, then shape into a ball, place in a bowl, cover, and let rise at room temperature for 1 hour.

Knead in the olives and the seeds and divide the dough into 8 to 10 equal portions. Shape each portion into a disk and place on parchment-lined baking sheets. Allow to rise at room temperature for 2 hours.

Preheat the oven to 425°F (220°C).

Bake the focaccia for 5 minutes, then reduce the oven temperature to 350°F (180°C) and bake until golden, an additional 5 to 7 minutes.

Stuffed Cabbage with Cannellini Puree

Many of you ask me for dishes that are quick and easy and can be made in advance and use seasonal produce. Here's one! These little bundles are delicious.

SERVES 4

½ head (400 g) cabbage
1 cup (250 g) canned cannellini, drained and rinsed
¼ cup plus 2 tablespoons (50 g) capers, rinsed and drained
Pepper
Extra-virgin olive oil

Separate the cabbage into leaves. Bring a large pot of water to a boil and blanch the leaves until tender, 7 to 8 minutes, taking care not to tear them. Drain and cool. If you want to make bite-sized stuffed cabbage, cut the leaves in half.

In a blender, puree the beans, capers, a pinch of pepper, and a drizzle of olive oil.

Spread a little of the bean filling in the center of one of the cooled cabbage leaves and fold the leaf around the filling. Repeat with remaining leaves and filling.

Serve at room temperature. You can also tie each packet with a chive for a pretty effect.

Make miniature stuffed cabbage!

P.S. Cabbage is economical and you can use every part of it. It stays good for a long time. Mince the less attractive outer leaves and cook them with minced onion as the base for risotto. The prettiest leaves are great for stuffed cabbage, and the rest can go into a soup made with barley, cannellini, carrots, and leeks.

Pan dei Morti Cookies

Pan dei morti are chocolate cookies traditionally made in Italy for All Soul's Day (aka Day of the Dead) on November 2. This is my version.

MAKES 8 TO 10 COOKIES

3 tablespoons (40 g) muscovado sugar

¾ cup (100 g) almonds

¾ cup plus 1 tablespoon (100 g) white whole wheat flour or Italian "tipo 2" flour

1 tablespoon unsweetened cocoa powder

½ teaspoon baking powder

1 teaspoon mixed ground spices including one or more of the following: cardamom, cinnamon, cloves, coriander

3½ ounces (100 g) large dates (about 4), pitted

2 tablespoons organic corn oil

About ¼ cup plus 3 tablespoons (100 ml) soy milk

1 tablespoon organic powdered sugar

Preheat the oven to 350°F (180°C). Line a baking sheet with parchment paper.

In a food processor, grind the muscovado sugar and almonds to a powder. Add the flour, cocoa powder, baking powder, mixed spices, and dates and grind to a paste.

Transfer the mixture to a large bowl. Beat in the oil and then gradually add the soy milk until you have a soft dough. You may not need all of the soy milk.

Use a tablespoon to place portions of the dough on the prepared pan and shape them into ovals. Bake until lightly browned, 15 to 20 minutes.

Remove the cookies from pan and allow them to cool. Sprinkle with the powdered sugar once they are cool.

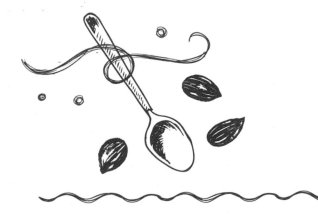

{ BASKET Nº 7 }

 Sun-Dried Tomatoes, Frozen Baby Peas, Salmon, Fresh Tomatoes, Whole-Grain Durum Flour

RECIPES

Home-Style Cake + Variation ———————————— 129
Pea and Mint Mousse on Toast + Variations ———— 130
Tube Cake with Yogurt Sauce + Variation ————— 133
Roasted Cherry Tomatoes with Onions
   + Variation ——————————————————————— 134
Pasta with Arugula Pesto and
   Crispy Salmon + Variation ————————————— 137
Pizza + Variation ————————————————————— 140
Mediterranean Bruschetta —————————————— 143

Home-Style Cake

This is the sort of humble plain cake that goes well with a bit of fruit preserves or yogurt or a glass of milk. This is a cake I made on the spur of the moment with what I had on hand, and you should feel free to approach it in the same spirit.

✓ **MAKES ONE 9-INCH (23-CM) CAKE/8 SERVINGS**

¾ cup (120 g) finely ground cornmeal

¾ cup (150 g) finely ground whole-grain durum flour

¼ cup (30 g) buckwheat flour

1 tablespoon baking powder

¼ cup plus 2 tablespoons (70 g) muscovado sugar

Firmly packed ⅓ cup (60 g) raisins

½ cup (60 g) chopped walnuts

3 tablespoons (40 ml) organic corn oil

¾ cup (180 ml) milk

Preheat the oven to 350°F (180°C). Line the bottom of a 9-inch (23-cm) cake pan with a round of parchment paper.

In a large bowl, combine the cornmeal, flours, baking powder, and sugar. Add the raisins and walnuts and toss with the dry ingredients. Add the corn oil and milk and stir to combine.

Pour the batter into the prepared pan and bake until a tester comes out clean, about 30 minutes.

Variation

Because it's not overly rich, it's perfect for breakfast. Try slicing it in half horizontally to make two layers and filling it with about ½ cup (150 g) of your favorite fruit preserves or 1 cup (250 g) ricotta whipped with a couple of tablespoons of honey.

Pea and Mint Mousse on Toast

If you use a good, satisfying whole wheat bread, a couple of slices of this and lunch is done!

✓ **MAKES 6 TOASTS**

1⅔ cups (250 g) frozen baby peas
15 fresh mint leaves
2 ounces (50 g) goat cheese
1 tablespoon plus 2 teaspoons (25 ml) mild-flavored extra-virgin olive oil
Salt and pepper
6 slices whole wheat bread, toasted

In a saucepan of boiling water, blanch the peas. Drain and transfer to a food processor.

Set aside 6 mint leaves for garnish and add the remaining 9 leaves to the peas in the food processor along with the goat cheese, oil, and a pinch each of salt and pepper. Puree the pea mixture until creamy. If necessary, add water in very small amounts to thin to a spreadable consistency. You won't need more than 2 tablespoons.

Spread the mixture on the toast and garnish each toast with a mint leaf.

Variations

Use the same amount of fava beans or edamame in place of the peas.

#tasteandhealth

Use COFFEE as an anti-inflammatory? Why not! Caffeine begins to circulate within thirty minutes of being ingested and is 99 percent absorbed within one hour. It peaks two hours after you drink it and has a half-life of two and a half to four and a half hours.

Coffee protects your heart and stops some kinds of tumors from forming, and it has anti-inflammatory powers that seem to be connected to its polyphenol content—and in particular the chlorogenic acid it contains. Caffeine influences the gastrointestinal system by increasing the secretion of hydrochloric acid and pepsin in the stomach, so it's not for those who suffer from gastritis or ulcers. However, caffeine does not cause reflux, gastritis, or ulcers in healthy people.

Tube Cake with Yogurt Sauce

✓ MAKES ONE TUBE CAKE/
ABOUT 8 SERVINGS

CAKE

Corn oil and flour, for the pan
1 cup (120 g) all-purpose flour
⅔ cup (80 g) whole wheat flour
½ cup (80 g) potato starch
¼ cup plus 2 tablespoons (80 g)
    muscovado sugar
¾ cup (100 g) almonds, chopped
1 tablespoon baking powder
⅓ cup (80 ml) organic corn oil
1 cup (250 ml) milk
Finely grated zest of 2 organic lemons

TOPPING

1 cup (300 g) Greek yogurt
2 tablespoons organic powdered sugar
½ pint (150 g) raspberries

Preheat the oven to 350°F (170°C). Lightly oil and flour an 8-inch (20-cm) tube pan.

FOR THE CAKE: In a bowl, combine the flours, potato starch, sugar, almonds, and baking powder. Stir in the oil, milk, and lemon zest. Mix briskly to incorporate as much air as possible.

Pour the batter into the prepared pan and bake until lightly browned, about 40 minutes. Cool the cake in the pan.

MEANWHILE, FOR THE TOPPING: In a small bowl, whisk together the yogurt and powdered sugar.

Serve wedges of the cake with the yogurt sauce on top and garnished with raspberries.

Variation

✓ MAKES ONE TUBE CAKE/
ABOUT 8 SERVINGS

Corn oil and flour, for the pan
1 cup (120 g) all-purpose flour
⅔ cup (80 g) whole wheat flour
½ cup (80 g) potato starch
1 tablespoon unsweetened cocoa powder
¼ cup plus 2 tablespoons (80 g)
    muscovado sugar
½ cup (80 g) hazelnuts, chopped
1 tablespoon baking powder
⅓ cup (80 ml) organic corn oil
1 cup (250 ml) almond milk or soy milk
Generous ½ cup (80 g) chocolate chips

Chocolate-Hazelnut Tube Cake

Preheat the oven to 350°F (170°C). Lightly oil and flour an 8-inch (20-cm) tube pan. In a bowl, combine the flours, potato starch, cocoa powder, sugar, hazelnuts, and baking powder. Stir in the oil, almond milk, and chocolate chips. Mix briskly to incorporate as much air as possible.

Pour the batter into the prepared pan and bake until lightly browned, about 40 minutes. Cool the cake in the pan.

Roasted Cherry Tomatoes with Onions

Red onions are a great ally in the fight against inflammation because they contain a significant amount of quercetin, an anti-oxidant that helps to rid the body of unwanted substances. These tomatoes are wonderful on toasted bread or used as a sauce for whole-wheat pasta.

✓ SERVES 4

1 pound (500 g) cherry tomatoes
2 red Tropea onions (Italian torpedo onions), or 1 medium red onion, cut into wedges
Oregano and/or rosemary sprigs
Extra-virgin olive oil
Salt and pepper

Preheat the oven to 425°F (220°C).

Halve the tomatoes and arrange in a baking pan. Add the onion wedges and scatter on the herbs. Drizzle with oil and season with salt and pepper.

Roast until the tomatoes and onions are lightly browned, about 20 minutes.

Variation

If you like, you can also toss the tomatoes with a few anchovy fillets or a few small balls of buffalo mozzarella just before serving.

Before

After

Pasta with Arugula Pesto and Crispy Salmon

I "stole" this first course from friends who made it for me at their house. It won me over from the first bite.

✓ **SERVES 4**

Salt
12 ounces (340 g) whole wheat farfalle pasta
6 cups (150 g) arugula
¼ cup (60 ml) extra-virgin olive oil
⅔ cup (100 g) feta cheese
14 ounces (400 g) salmon fillet
¼ cup plus 3 tablespoons (100 ml) orange juice
¼ cup (30 g) oil-packed sun-dried tomatoes, drained and minced
¼ cup (30 g) hemp hearts
¼ cup (30 g) chopped pistachios

In a large pot of lightly salted boiling water, cook the pasta to al dente. Drain and cool under running water. Return to the cooking pot.

In a food processor or blender, combine the arugula, oil, and feta and puree. Add a tablespoon or two of water to make a creamy pesto.

In a dry nonstick skillet over high heat, add the salmon, sprinkle lightly with salt and cook for 2 minutes per side. Add the orange juice and cook until the juice has evaporated and the surface of the fish is crispy and caramelized.

Add the arugula pesto to the pasta and toss to coat. Add a couple of tablespoons of water and reheat briefly.

Transfer the pasta to individual plates and top each portion with slices of the salmon. Garnish with the minced sun-dried tomatoes, hemp hearts, and pistachios.

Variation

If desired, replace the arugula with baby spinach.

#tasteandhealth

Watch out for animal fats and some vegetable fats, such as peanut oil, that are high in ARACHIDONIC ACID, which causes INFLAMMATION. That's why the magic word when it comes to eating meat (especially red meat), cold cuts, and eggs is "moderation." Fatty fish and plant foods can be eaten in abundance, though, because they help fight inflammation.

Even dairy products contain arachidonic acid, but they supply important nutrients such as calcium and vitamin D. Your best bet is to eat low-fat and nonfat dairy products (1.5 percent fat at most) and cheeses that are 45 percent fat at most. The lower the fat content, the less arachidonic acid they contain.

#tasteandhealth

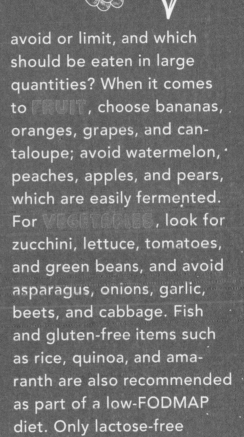

FODMAP is an acronym that stands for "Fermentable Oligosaccharides, Disaccharides, Monosaccharides, and Polyols." That's a mouthful that simply means SUGARS WITH A TENDENCY TO FERMENT (fructose, lactose, fructans, xylitol).

A diet high in these sugars can exacerbate the most common symptoms of IRRITABLE BOWEL SYNDROME, or IBS (bloating, gas, abdominal pain, irregularity). A University of Michigan study published in *Gastroenterology* showed that a low-FODMAP diet reduces those symptoms.

When IBS is in the acute phase, it's a good idea to follow a low-FODMAP diet for a while.

What are the foods to avoid or limit, and which should be eaten in large quantities? When it comes to FRUIT, choose bananas, oranges, grapes, and cantaloupe; avoid watermelon, peaches, apples, and pears, which are easily fermented. For VEGETABLES, look for zucchini, lettuce, tomatoes, and green beans, and avoid asparagus, onions, garlic, beets, and cabbage. Fish and gluten-free items such as rice, quinoa, and amaranth are also recommended as part of a low-FODMAP diet. Only lactose-free DAIRY PRODUCTS are permitted.

Keep in mind, however, that a low-FODMAP diet should not be followed for an extended period and any eliminated foods should gradually be reintroduced.

Pizza

Not a week goes by that I don't serve pizza for lunch or dinner. The common denominator all my pizzas share? Lots of vegetables, a small amount of cheese, and plenty of sauce!

SERVES 4 TO 6

½ teaspoon active dry yeast or ⅙ cake (3 g) compressed fresh yeast

1 cup plus 2 tablespoons (267 ml) warm water

3 cups (380 g) all-purpose flour

1 cup (120 g) whole wheat flour

Scant 2 tablespoons (25 g) extra-virgin olive oil, plus more for drizzling

½ teaspoon (10 g) salt

¼ cup (about 50 g) tomato sauce

Grilled peppers, or other cooked vegetables, to taste

Dissolve the yeast in ¼ cup (60 ml) of the warm water. In a large bowl, combine the flours and olive oil. Stir in the yeast mixture, then gradually knead in enough warm water to make a smooth dough. Knead in the salt. Shape the dough into a ball, transfer it to a large bowl or container, cover tightly, and let rise on the lowest shelf of the refrigerator for 24 hours.

Preheat the oven to 425°F (220°). Line a 9-inch (23-cm) sheet pan with parchment paper.

Remove the dough from the refrigerator and with your hands press it into the prepared pan. Let the dough rest at room temperature for 30 minutes.

Top with the tomato sauce and grilled peppers (or other vegetables of your choosing) and drizzle on a little olive oil. Bake for about 20 minutes.

Variation

SERVES 4 TO 6
GLUTEN-FREE PIZZA CRUST

1 head cauliflower, broken into florets

Salt and pepper

3 tablespoons extra-virgin olive oil

2 egg whites

¼ cup (about 50 g) tomato sauce

Preheat the oven to 400°F (200°C). Line a 9-inch (23-cm) sheet pan with parchment paper.

In a food processor, grind the cauliflower to a fine rice. Mix in a pinch of salt, the oil, and egg whites. Press the cauliflower about ¾ inch deep into the prepared pan.

Bake about 30 minutes. Spread on tomato sauce and toppings of your choice. Bake as above.

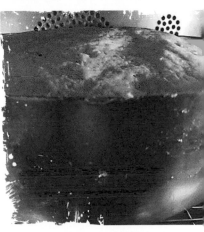

Mediterranean Bruschetta

Vivienne loves this so much that she adds herbs. In addition to the oregano? You bet. Never get in the way of an ambitious kid in the kitchen!

✓ **SERVES 6**

2¼ cups (250 g) oil-packed sun-dried tomatoes, drained

½ cup (100 ml) tomato puree

1 tablespoon plus 1 teaspoon muscovado sugar

Pinch of dried oregano

¼ cup (30 g) chopped red onion

2 tablespoons capers, rinsed and drained

1 tablespoon plus 2 teaspoons mild-flavored extra-virgin olive oil

6 slices whole wheat bread, toasted

Slice 4 to 5 sun-dried tomatoes and set aside for garnish.

In a blender or food processor, combine the remaining sun-dried tomatoes, the tomato puree, sugar, oregano, red onion, capers, and olive oil and process into a smooth mixture.

Spread the mixture on the bread. Garnish with the reserved strips of sun-dried tomato.

P.S. You can also serve the pureed mixture over barley or farro. Either is a delicious pairing!

Use this sauce on barley or farro!

{ BASKET № 8 }

**Lentils,
Ricotta, Quinoa,
Mushrooms, Spinach,
Cauliflower**

RECIPES

Tagliatelle with Mushrooms and
   Ricotta-Pumpkin Cream ————————————— 147
Seasonal Autumn Quinoa ————————————— 148
Lentil Salad ————————————————————— 149
Cauliflower Pasta + Variations ———————————— 150
Extra-Light Apple Cake ——————————————— 153
Cream of Cauliflower, Celery Root, and
   Greek Yogurt Soup ————————————————— 154
Green Pasta —————————————————————— 157

Tagliatelle with Mushrooms and Ricotta-Pumpkin Cream

I made this on TV with the wonderful Antonella Clerici. Everybody loved it, and I hope you'll love it, too.

SERVES 4

- 11 ounces (300 g) peeled and seeded winter squash, such as pumpkin, kabocha, or kuri (about ½ medium squash), cut into cubes
- 1 shallot, minced
- Generous 1 cup (250 g) Italian-style ricotta cheese or well-drained regular ricotta
- 1 tablespoon plus 1 teaspoon extra-virgin olive oil
- Salt and pepper
- 1¾ ounces (50 g) sliced dried porcini mushrooms (about 14)
- 5 ounces (150 g) white button mushrooms, sliced
- 11 ounces (320 g) dried egg tagliatelle
- 10 fresh chives, minced

In a large skillet, sauté the squash and shallot in a little water until the squash is soft. Transfer the squash and shallot to a food processor, add the ricotta and drizzle in some oil, and puree. Season with salt and pepper.

Soak the dried mushrooms in water for about 15 minutes. Carefully scoop them out of the water, leaving any grit behind in the bowl. Drain the mushrooms well. In a skillet, heat a little oil over medium heat. Add the dried mushrooms and the fresh mushrooms and season with salt and pepper. Do not add any water to the pan as the mushrooms will give off plenty. Cook until done. Set aside.

In a large pot of lightly salted boiling water, cook the pasta until al dente. Drain and cool under running water. Return to the cooking pot.

Add the ricotta-pumpkin cream, mushrooms, and chives to the pasta and toss to combine. Reheat briefly with an additional drizzle of olive oil and serve.

P.S. This sauce is also great on whole wheat pasta or buckwheat noodles (pizzoccheri).

Seasonal Autumn Quinoa

Quinoa is rich in protein, calcium, and good fat. If you don't have a taste for it, you can use couscous here instead.

✓ SERVES 4

2 cups (320 g) quinoa, rinsed

1 pound (500 g) broccoli, broken into florets

Leaves of 3 sprigs parsley

¾ cup (80 g) oil-packed sun-dried tomatoes, drained

1 cup (150 g) pitted Taggiasca or Niçoise olives

3 carrots, finely diced

Extra-virgin olive oil

Finely grated zest and juice of 1 organic lemon

In a saucepan, bring 4 cups (950 ml) water to a boil. Add the quinoa, cover, and cook until the water is absorbed, about 20 minutes. Halfway through, add the broccoli.

Meanwhile, on a cutting board, mince together the parsley, sun-dried tomatoes, and olives.

When the quinoa is cooked, fluff it with a fork, cover, and let sit for about 5 minutes, then turn out into a large bowl to cool slightly. Add the carrots and the parsley mixture and toss together. Dress with a little olive oil, lemon zest, and lemon juice.

Lentil Salad

I suggest preparing large batches of lentils and freezing them. The freezer is great for storing both legumes and cooked grains.

✓ SERVES 4

1¼ cups (250 g) lentils
¾ cup (80 g) oil-packed sun-dried tomatoes, drained
1 leek, trimmed
Leaves of 1 bunch parsley
Extra-virgin olive oil
Juice of 1 lemon
¼-inch (½-cm) piece fresh ginger, grated

In a large saucepan of lightly salted boiling water, cook the lentils until firm-tender, about 20 minutes. Drain well and transfer to a bowl.

On a cutting board, mince together the sun-dried tomatoes, leek, and parsley—all uncooked—and toss with the lentils.

Before serving, drizzle in some oil, add the lemon juice and fresh ginger, and toss well.

P.S. You can switch up the ingredients here as you like, but always use lemon juice because it helps you absorb the iron in the sun-dried tomatoes and lentils.

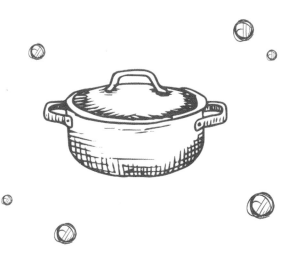

Cauliflower Pasta

This incredible first course is made in advance and then reheated in a skillet or warmed in the oven.

SERVES 4

⅓ cup (50 g) raisins
Fresh parsley leaves, to taste
⅔ cup (70 g) walnuts
1 yellow onion
4 oil-packed anchovy fillets, drained
Extra-virgin olive oil
Red pepper flakes
1 head cauliflower, trimmed
Salt
12 ounces (320 g) whole wheat pasta

Place the raisins in a small bowl and add water to cover. Set aside to soak for 15 minutes. Drain the raisins and squeeze them dry.

On a cutting board, mince together the parsley, walnuts, onion, and anchovies.

In a skillet, cook the anchovy mixture with a little oil and red pepper flakes to taste over very low heat until the anchovies have dissolved.

In a large pot of boiling unsalted water, cook the whole head of cauliflower, about 20 minutes. Drain and break into florets.

Transfer about 10 cooked cauliflower florets to a food processor and puree until smooth, then add the puree to the anchovy mixture in the skillet.

In a large pot of lightly salted boiling water, cook the pasta until al dente. Drain and toss with the cauliflower-anchovy mixture and the remaining cauliflower florets.

Variations

You can use Romanesco in place of the cauliflower, or try Brussels sprouts or purple cauliflower.

#tasteandhealth

VITAMIN C is found in more than just citrus. So many foods contain vitamin C. Want a few figures? The daily recommended dose of vitamin C is 60 milligrams (mg). The juice of ½ lemon contains 22 mg; about ¼ cup (100 g) of arugula contains 15 mg; ¾ cup (150 g) of strawberries has 80 mg; a medium tomato contains 50 mg; a quarter pound (100 g) of raw bell peppers has four times as much as an orange; And speaking of oranges, by weight raw cauliflower provides more vitamin C than an orange does. So try some as a crudité dipped in olive oil, salt, pepper, and mustard powder! You'll keep coming back for more!

Extra-Light Apple Cake

An apple cake smells like home. To me, there's nothing like it. An apple cake means family, memories, and love.

MAKES ONE 9-INCH (23-CM) CAKE/8 SERVINGS

2 cups (250 g) whole wheat flour

3 tablespoons plus 1 teaspoon (40 g) stevia

1 tablespoon baking powder

Grated zest and juice of 1 organic lemon

½ cup plus 3 tablespoons (200 ml) milk

3 tablespoons plus 1 teaspoon (50 ml) extra-virgin olive oil

⅓ cup (70 g) dried apricots, finely chopped

1 pound (500 g) apples, peeled and diced

Preheat the oven to 350°F (180°C). Line the bottom of a 9-inch (23-cm) cake pan with a round of parchment paper.

In a large bowl, combine the flour, stevia, baking powder, and lemon zest. Stir in the milk, olive oil, and lemon juice. Fold in the dried apricots and apples.

Scrape the batter into the prepared pan and bake until lightly browned, about 45 minutes.

P.S. This recipe was created for a diabetic child so it contains no added sugar. You can add some ground cinnamon to enhance the flavor.

Cream of Cauliflower, Celery Root, and Greek Yogurt Soup

This humble recipe was created on a whim but has become one of my mainstays. It's an excellent opener to a dinner with friends.

✓ **SERVES 4**

14 ounces (400 g) peeled celery root, cut into big chunks

14 ounces (400 g) cauliflower florets (from about 1 medium head)

Generous ¾ cup (9 oz/250 g) 0% Greek yogurt

Extra-virgin olive oil

Salt and pepper

Saffron, for garnish

In a saucepan, combine the celery root, cauliflower, and water just to cover. Bring to a boil and cook until soft. Drain, transfer to a food processor, and puree into a smooth cream with no lumps.

Add the yogurt and a drizzle of olive oil and puree until smooth. Season with salt and pepper.

Divide among individual serving dishes and garnish with saffron.

#tasteandhealth

Let's talk about WATER misconceptions. Depending on where you live, some tap water systems contain lime buildup. The taste may bother some people, but it's nothing more than calcium carbonate, meaning it's a good source of calcium. Ingesting it won't cause you to develop kidney stones or gallstones—those are made of calcium oxalate. You only need to eschew tap water if you're a clothing iron. (Calcium carbonate ruins metal, but that's it!)

Another thing that strikes fear in the hearts of many is the term TOTAL DISSOLVED SOLIDS (TDS) that appears on some bottles of mineral water. That phrase doesn't indicate anything bad or negative. It's just a technical term that shows the MINERAL CONTENT that remains after a liter of water evaporates at 356°F (180°C).

Water with a high TDS number is richer in minerals than water with a low number. That's all. For specific dietary concerns, consult your doctor to recommend the best water for you.

Green Pasta

It doesn't cost much and we buy a lot of it. I'm talking about spinach, of course. If you don't know what to do with it, I've got you covered: Here's the dish for you. I created this recipe when Veru was pregnant. Since spinach (like all leafy greens) is rich in folate, I took raw tender baby spinach and turned it into a sauce. There's no law against blanching the spinach for a moment before pureeing it!

✓ SERVES 4

Salt
12 ounces (320 g) buckwheat pasta (pizzoccheri)
4 ounces (100 g) baby spinach (3 to 4 cups)
1 cup (120 g) walnuts
3 ounces (80 g) Quartirolo Lombardo or feta cheese
Extra-virgin olive oil

In a large pot of lightly salted boiling water, cook the pasta until al dente.

Meanwhile, in a food processor, combine the spinach, walnuts, cheese, and a little bit of olive oil until smooth and creamy. Add water in small amounts if needed to reach the right consistency.

Drain the pasta and toss with the sauce.

P.S. Buckwheat is gluten-free and high in protein, fiber, and minerals. But if you have whole wheat pasta and want to use that instead, I won't be upset ;-) and the dish will taste just as good!

{ BASKET Nº 9 }

Almonds, Tomatoes, Fresh Apricots, Bell Peppers, Ricotta, Cucumbers

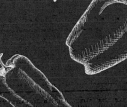

RECIPES

Classic Gazpacho + Alternative _____ 160
Apricot and Mango Salad _____ 163
Buckwheat Noodles Trapani-Style _____ 164
Cucumber Water + Variations _____ 167
Ricotta Spoon Sweet _____ 168
Apricot Cake _____ 169
Detox Juice _____ 170

Classic Gazpacho

Gazpacho is a powerhouse full of vitamin C, carotenoids, quercetin, fiber, and anthocyanins. In short, it's a concentrated burst of taste and health.

✓ **SERVES 4**

2 red onions
1 mango
4 tomatoes
2 cucumbers
2 bell peppers (1 red, 1 green)
Tabasco sauce
Juice of ½ lemon
5 tablespoons extra-virgin olive oil
4 cups (1 liter) tomato puree
Salt and pepper
Whole wheat bread, toasted

Mince the onions and place in a bowl. Dice the mango, tomatoes, cucumbers, and bell peppers and add to the bowl. Add Tabasco sauce to taste, the lemon juice, and olive oil. Toss to combine. Add the tomato puree and season with salt and pepper. Refrigerate for 2 hours before serving.

Serve with whole wheat toast.

Alternative

✓ **SERVES 4**

6 small cucumbers
1 white onion, cut into chunks
9 ounces (250 g) baby spinach
    (7 to 8 cups)
2 cups (50 g) basil leaves
¾ cup (20 g) parsley leaves
2 Italian frying peppers, cut into chunks
3 tablespoons (50 g) 0% Greek yogurt
⅔ cup (150 ml) extra-virgin olive oil, plus
    more for drizzling
1 teaspoon muscovado sugar
Salt and pepper
Whole wheat bread, toasted

Green Gazpacho

Peel and chunk the cucumbers and place them in a food processor. Add the onion, spinach, basil, parsley, and frying peppers and process. After a few minutes add the yogurt, the ⅔ cup (150 ml) oil, the sugar, and salt and pepper to taste. Process again until the mixture is bright green.

Refrigerate for 2 hours before serving.

Divide the soup among bowls and drizzle on additional oil. Serve with the toast.

Green

Classic

#tasteandhealth

Scientists have discovered that eating SOY AND SOY PRODUCTS such as tofu and (unsweetened) soy milk provides a variety of benefits, from fighting cancer to lowering LDL ("bad") cholesterol: Regular soy consumption as part of a balanced and healthy diet can bring LDL down by 10 to 15 percent. Soy is 42 percent protein, making it one of the best sources of plant protein. Soybeans (mature soybeans as well as green edamame), tofu, and tempeh provide the most benefits, while soy milk is less effective, and soy sauce—a very salty seasoning—offers none.

Apricot and Mango Salad

We should all work to incorporate fruit into our meals. It's not an extra but an important part of a daily diet. So go ahead and add lots of tasty fruit to your salads!

✓ **SERVES 4**

6 fresh apricots
3 tablespoons extra-virgin olive oil, plus more for sauteeing
3 tablespoons fresh lemon juice
1 teaspoon honey
5 fresh mint leaves
Pinch of salt
9 ounces (250 g) arugula (10 to 12 cups)
3½ oz (100 g) butterhead lettuce (about ½ head)
1 mango, diced
1 Granny Smith apple, peeled (if not organic) and diced
1⅔ cups (250 g) crumbled feta cheese

Briefly warm the apricots, cut in half without the stones, in a skillet with olive oil until lightly sauteed, then cut them into wedges.

In a mini food processor, blend the lemon juice, oil, honey, mint, and salt to combine.

Tear the arugula and lettuce leaves by hand and make a bed of the two on a large serving platter. Arrange the apricots, mango, and apple on top and sprinkle with the feta cheese. Drizzle on the dressing and serve!

Buckwheat Noodles Trapani-Style

My favorite dishes? Pizza (whole wheat crust, lots of vegetables, tomato sauce), hummus, pasta (whole wheat with tomato sauce topped with feta or aged ricotta), and . . . pizzoccheri, cooked my way!

✓ **SERVES 4**

Salt

12 ounces (320 g) pizzoccheri (Italian buckwheat noodles)

½ cup (50 g) whole wheat breadcrumbs

½ cup (50 g) almonds

5 oil-packed sun-dried tomatoes, drained

5 fresh tomatoes, diced

10 basil leaves

½ to 1 clove garlic, to taste

Extra-virgin olive oil

Black pepper to taste

In a large pot of lightly salted boiling water, cook the pizzoccheri.

Meanwhile, in a nonstick skillet, toast the breadcrumbs. In a food processor, combine the toasted breadcrumbs, almonds, sun-dried tomatoes, fresh tomatoes, basil, garlic, and a few tablespoons of olive oil. Puree until creamy.

When the pizzoccheri are ready, drain them and rinse under running water. Toss with the pesto. Transfer them to a skillet, drizzle with a little olive oil, and reheat. Season with pepper before serving.

Pizzoccheri are one of my favorites. I love them with anything and everything!

Cucumber Water

Cool. Refreshing. That's how I'd describe my favorite flavored water, made with cucumber, lemon, and ginger!

✓ **SERVES 6 TO 8**

One 2-quart (2-liter) bottle
    sparkling water
2 cucumbers, thinly sliced
10 fresh mint leaves
1 organic lime
1 organic lemon
⅓-inch (1-cm) piece fresh ginger

Place the sparkling water in a pitcher. Slice the cucumbers and add them to the water along with the mint leaves. Thinly slice the lime and lemon and add those as well. Peel the ginger, cut it into small dice, and add to the water. Let this beverage infuse in the refrigerator for at least 3 hours before serving. It must be well chilled!

You can create your own favorite flavored water with the ingredients you love!

P.S. It looks really "fancy" if you freeze the lemon and lime slices. That way they both cool down the drink and flavor it!

Variations

You can create your own favorites! One piece of advice: Think seasonally. In summer use peaches, strawberries, and ginger for an excellent flavored water.

In winter you can make an infusion: Bring water to a boil and let the flavoring elements steep for 15 to 20 minutes.

My winter favorite? Ginger, 1 organic lemon, and 1 bay leaf in 2 quarts (2 liters) of water.

Ricotta Spoon Sweet

This is a dessert for coddling friends, family, and, obviously, yourself. Because cooking is an act of love!

✓ **SERVES 4**

3 egg whites

2½ cups (500 g) Italian-style ricotta cheese or well-drained regular ricotta

25 (150 g) amaretti cookies, crumbled

5 fresh apricots

2 ounces (50 g) dark chocolate (72% cacao)

In a bowl, with an electric mixer, whip the egg whites to stiff peaks. Fold in the ricotta and the crumbled cookies. Work very gently to avoid deflating the egg whites. Transfer to individual serving dishes.

Pit and slice the apricots and arrange them on top, then grate chocolate onto each bowl.

Refrigerate for 5 hours before serving.

P.S. Out of eggs? Simply leave out the egg whites. The dessert will still taste great!

Apricot Cake

Somebody's birthday? An anniversary? This cake—so versatile and so good—is the perfect solution. This isn't a cake that rises very high, but the sweet and sour flavor from the apricots is fantastic.

✓ **MAKES ONE 9-INCH (23-CM) CAKE/6 TO 8 SERVINGS**

1½ cups (190 g) all-purpose flour
½ cup (60 g) whole wheat flour
¼ cup (50 g) muscovado sugar
1 tablespoon baking powder
½ cup plus 3 tablespoons (200 ml) milk
¼ cup (60 ml) organic corn oil
10 fresh apricots, pitted and finely diced

Preheat the oven to 350°F (180°C). Line the bottom of a 9-inch (23-cm) cake pan with a round of parchment paper.

In a large bowl, combine the flours, sugar, baking powder, milk, and oil. Fold the apricots into the batter.

Pour the batter into the prepared pan. Bake until lightly browned, 40 to 45 minutes.

P.S. It's best to serve this with 1 cup (250 g) yogurt whipped with 3 tablespoons (60 g) apricot preserves. So delicious! Try replacing the milk with unsweetened soy milk and adding melted chocolate, but it must be 72% cacao dark chocolate.

Detox Juice

I use an extraction juicer to make juice because it is gentler with the fruit than a centrifugal juicer or a blender. It treats the fruits and vegetables tenderly and preserves their nutritional value.

✓ SERVES 2

2 cucumbers
1 Granny Smith apple
½ mango
1 pineapple

Extract the juice from all the ingredients and drink chilled! You can also dilute the juice with a little sparkling water.

P.S. If drinking fruit isn't enough, eat it, too!

Combine any leftover fruit with endive, mâche, and a tablespoon of mustard. It's the perfect salad!

Or eat any leftover fruit with almonds or walnuts or dress with a teaspoon of a mild-flavored extra-virgin olive oil in order to better absorb the carotenoids from the mango.

If you have fruit left over, use it to make a delicious salad!

{ BASKET № 10 }

**Black Rice, Farro,
Radicchio,
Milk,
Sun-Dried Tomatoes,
Lentils**

RECIPES

Black Rice with Lentils _____ 174
Pasta with Radicchio Sauce + Variation _____ 177
Farro and Chickpea Soup + Variation _____ 178
Radicchio and Apple Salad _____ 180
Farro Blancmange + Variation _____ 181
Radicchio Stuffed with Tofu and
    Anchovy Mousse + Variation _____ 182

Black Rice with Lentils

This is a fantastic one-dish meal full of fiber; minerals such as iron, manganese, copper, and magnesium; vitamins; protein; and functional molecules, which benefit the cardiovascular system.

✓ SERVES 4

1¾ cups (320 g) black rice
Leaves of 1 bunch parsley
¾ cup (80 g) oil-packed sun-dried tomatoes, drained
¾ cup (80 g) walnuts
1 cup (200 g) cooked lentils
Grated zest and juice of 1 organic lemon
5 tablespoons extra-virgin olive oil

In a saucepan, combine the rice with 3 cups (700 ml) water, cover with a tight-fitting lid, and cook over low heat for 20 minutes. Remove the pan from the heat and let the rice continue to steam, covered, until fully cooked, about 15 additional minutes.

Meanwhile, chop together the parsley, sun-dried tomatoes, and walnuts to make a quick sauce.

Add the lentils, lemon zest, lemon juice, and olive oil to the cooked rice. Finally, add the sauce.

P.S. Black rice, brown rice: Pick whatever you like best. They're all packed with fiber!

You can also use basmati rice. Long-grain rice like basmati is less starchy and therefore better for your health!

#tasteandhealth

ANTHOCYANINS (purple, blue, and dark red pigments), ellagitannins, proanthocyanidins, and phenolic acids (such as chlorogenic acid) are some of the most beneficial substances for your health. Blueberries, blackberries, eggplant, plums, red grapes, beets, and radicchio all have them!

These substances are part of the polyphenol family, and polyphenols help prevent chronic degenerative disease. And that's not all—they're antioxidants that have benefits for healthy people as well as those with risk factors for degenerative diseases.

One epidemiology study conducted for sixteen years on 34,489 post-menopausal American women demonstrated that a diet rich in flavonoids, and especially anthocyanins, reduces the risk of death due to cardiovascular disease. There are other solid studies that show that anthocyanins regulate various biochemical pathways involved in the development of cardiovascular disease.

Pasta with Radicchio Sauce

Cashews, radicchio, onion, Quartirolo Lombardo cheese—what a fabulous group of ingredients. You won't believe how good they taste together!

✓ **SERVES 4**

1 head radicchio, cut into strips
1 yellow onion, minced
½ cup (80 g) unsalted cashews
5 tablespoons extra-virgin olive oil, plus more to drizzle
4 ounces (100 g) Quartirolo Lombardo or feta cheese
Salt and pepper
12 ounces (320 g) whole wheat pasta

In a skillet, sauté the radicchio and onion in a couple of tablespoons of water, stirring constantly. When the radicchio mixture is soft, transfer to a food processor and add the cashews, oil, and cheese and puree. Season to taste with salt and pepper, but don't overdo it on the salt. (Restrain yourself!)

In a large pot of lightly salted boiling water, cook the pasta until al dente, then rinse under running water.

Toss the pasta and radicchio sauce together and reheat in a skillet with an additional drizzle of extra-virgin olive oil.

Variation

For a different spin, replace the Quartirolo with smoked tofu and the salt with Niçoise or Taggiasca olives.

Farro and Chickpea Soup

Farro is an ancient variety of wheat. It's rich in fiber, but also in B vitamins, phosphorous, and potassium. This is a staple ingredient you should always have in your pantry!

✓ **SERVES 4**

1 carrot, minced
1 white onion, minced
1 stalk celery, minced
1¾ cups (320 g) farro
Extra-virgin olive oil, as a drizzle, to taste
2 sprigs rosemary
2 bay leaves
1 cup (250 g) canned chickpeas, drained and rinsed
Salt and pepper

In a soup pot, cook the carrot, onion, and celery in water (no oil) until softened, about 10 minutes.

Add the farro, oil, rosemary, and bay leaves and enough water to cover the farro. Bring to a boil and boil for 20 minutes. Add the chickpeas and additional water if needed, depending on the consistency you desire. Season to taste with salt and pepper.

After about 20 minutes, the soup is ready! Remove the bay leaves and rosemary sprigs before serving.

P.S. Not a fan of whole chickpeas? No problem—just puree the mixture before adding the farro.

Variation

Replace the farro with barley and use dried mushrooms in place of the chickpeas.

Radicchio and Apple Salad

This is an unusual salad. It offers a way to work lots of fruit into your meals. A great combination, a wonderful blend of flavors.

✓ **SERVES 4**

4 medium sweet potatoes
Juice of 1 lemon
1 Granny Smith apple
4 tablespoons raisins
1 head radicchio, slivered
⅔ cup (80 g) pitted Niçoise or Taggiasca olives, sliced
1 cup (150 g) crumbled feta cheese
¼ cup (60 ml) extra-virgin olive oil
½ cup (120 ml) balsamic vinegar

In a large pot of boiling unsalted water, cook the whole sweet potatoes until firm-tender. Drain and set aside to cool. When cool enough to handle, peel and cut into rounds.

Fill a medium bowl with water and add the lemon juice. Peel, core, and dice the apple. Add the cut apple pieces and the raisins to the acidulated water.

To compose the salad, start with a bed of the radicchio. Top with the sweet potatoes. Drain the apple and raisins and add. Then add the olives and feta.

Drizzle with the oil and balsamic vinegar.

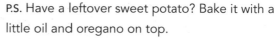

P.S. Have a leftover sweet potato? Bake it with a little oil and oregano on top.

To serve, crush lightly with a fork and accompany with goat cheese.

Farro Blancmange

This classic recipe is made of humble ingredients but has flavors fit for a king. It's an ideal dessert or snack and also a nice Sunday breakfast option.

✓ SERVES 4

1⅔ cups (300 g) farro

4 cups (1 liter) unsweetened almond milk

¾ cup (100 g) wheat starch

⅔ cup (80 g) organic powdered sugar

Finely grated zest of 1 organic lemon

1 cup (70 g) chopped candied orange peel

2 ounces (60 g) dark chocolate (72% cacao)

In a pot of boiling unsalted water, cook the farro to your desired density. Drain well.

In a large pot, whisk together the almond milk, wheat starch, sugar, and lemon zest. Place over medium heat. When the first bubbles appear, stir in the farro. Once the mixture has reached the desired consistency, remove from the heat, stir in the candied orange peel, and divide among individual serving dishes.

Let cool and then grate the chocolate on top. Store in the refrigerator.

Variation

For a gluten-free version, replace the farro with 1⅓ cups (300 g) semi-polished rice and use cornstarch in place of the wheat starch. That's all it takes! The method is exactly the same.

181

Radicchio Stuffed with Tofu and Anchovy Mousse

What I like to do in the kitchen is create dishes that are not only healthy, but also pretty and colorful.

✓ **SERVES 4**

1 head Treviso radicchio
10 ounces (300 g) tofu
1 ounce (30 g) oil-packed anchovy fillets (about 11), drained
Juice of 1 lemon
⅔ cup (80 g) pitted Niçoise or Taggiasca olives
¼ cup (60 ml) extra-virgin olive oil
Chives, for garnish

Break the head of radicchio into leaves and choose 16 of the largest, prettiest leaves.

In a food processor, blend the tofu with the anchovies, lemon juice, olives, and olive oil. With the machine running, drizzle in water in a thin stream until creamy, velvety, and delicious. The tofu will get creamy thanks to the water you're adding along with the other ingredients but it will take a few minutes.

Serve each radicchio leaf with a quenelle of the tofu mixture on top. Garnish with a chive.

Variation

Here's a vegan version: Replace the anchovies with ⅔ cup (70 g) drained oil-packed sun-dried tomatoes and reduce the olives to ½ cup (70 g).

THANK YOU!

There are many surprises in life. Really a lot. This has been an intense year with lots of changes, emotions, and choices. I'd like to thank my family: my mother, Cristina; my father, Umberto; Mirca and Gianni; my sister, Barbara; and especially my girls, Veruska and Vivienne.

Thank you to some special friends: Renato, Alberto, Igor, Taty, Alessandro, Martina, Kevin, Nico, Roberto, Simona, Filippo, Andrea, Romina, Mike, Alessandro, Sofia, Davide, Luca, Albino and Barbara, Federica and Oscar, Teresa, Silvia and Barbara, Patrizia—thank you from the bottom of my heart. Each of you knows why I'm thanking you. Finally, sincerest thanks to the Fondazione Veronesi, my splendid team at Realize Networks (Pasquale, Rosario, Serena, Claudia, Simone, Alessia, Giulia, Ivano, Salvo, Giada, Monica, Silvia, Alex), and my publisher, HarperCollins, who has made it possible to give you what you want, a book in color! Thank you so much—you're the best!

Index by DISH

APPETIZERS AND BREADS

Avocado Tartare with Lime and Red Onion _____ 92

Beet Chips _____ 86

Carrot-Yogurt Shots + Variation _____ 98

Green Toasts _____ 49

Mediterranean Bruschetta _____ 143

Mini Focaccia Breads with Seeds and Olives _____ 121

Pea and Mint Mousse on Toast + Variations _____ 130

Pizza + Variation _____ 140

Radicchio Stuffed with Tofu and
    Anchovy Mousse + Variation _____ 182

Roasted Cherry Tomatoes with Onions + Variation _____ 134

Savory Leek Tart + Variation _____ 70

SAUCES AND SPREADS

Eggless Mayonnaise + Variations _____ 43

Hummus + Variation _____ 88

Pea, Zucchini, and Goat Cheese Pesto + Variation _____ 78

Pumpkin and Chickpea Spread _____ 77

SOUPS

Cream of Cauliflower, Celery Root, and Greek Yogurt Soup__ 154

Classic Gazpacho + Alternative _____ 160

Pumpkin Soup with Ginger + Variation_____ 74

Farro and Chickpea Soup + Variation_____ 178

PASTA AND GRAINS

Barley Risotto-Style with Pepper and
   Goat Cheese Cream + Variation _____ 119

Black Rice with Lentils _____ 174

Buckwheat Noodles Trapani-Style _____ 164

Cauliflower Pasta + Variations _____ 150

Farro Blancmange + Variation_____ 181

Green Pasta _____ 157

Pasta with Arugula Pesto and Crispy Salmon + Variation ___ 137

Pasta with Eggplant, Taggiasca Olives, Capers, and Mint __ 108
Pasta with Radicchio Sauce + Variation _____ 177
Seasonal Autumn Quinoa _____ 148
Tagliatelle with Mushrooms and Ricotta-Pumpkin Cream __ 147

MAIN COURSES

Cannellini and Tuna "Meatballs" + Variations _____ 115
Crispy Anchovies with Lemon _____ 45
Eggless Leek Frittata _____ 73
Falafel _____ 51
Greek Chickpea and Zucchini
   "Meatballs" + Variations _____ 81
Mediterranean Sushi _____ 82
Stuffed Cabbage with Cannellini Puree _____ 122

SALADS

Apple-Walnut Salad with Balsamic-Honey Dressing _____ 60
Apricot and Mango Salad _____ 163
Chickpea, Celery, and Feta Salad + Variations _____ 91
Lentil Salad _____ 149
Lentil and Walnut Salad _____ 55
Radicchio and Apple Salad _____ 180

DESSERTS

Apricot Cake ———————————————— 169

Beet Cake ———————————————— 87

Carrot Muffins + Variation ———————————— 107

Chocolate Roll ———————————————— 101

Coconut Treats + Variations ———————————— 104

Crumble + Variations ———————————— 67

Extra-Light Apple Cake ———————————— 153

Gingerbread Men ———————————————— 116

Granola ———————————————— 56

Home-Style Cake + Variation ———————————— 129

Individual Chocolate Lava Cakes + Variations ————— 102

Kisses + Variation ———————————————— 59

Matcha Crêpes ———————————————— 110

Pan de Mej + Variations ———————————— 46

Pan dei Morti Cookies ———————————— 125

Pancakes with Bananas, Raspberries, and Honey ————— 64

Ricotta Berry Tartlets + Variations ——————— 63

Ricotta Spoon Sweet ———————————— 168

Tube Cake with Yogurt Sauce + Variation ————— 133

BEVERAGES

Celery, Apple, and Ginger Juice + Alternative ————— 95

Cucumber Water + Variations ———————————— 167

Detox Juice ———————————————— 170

Index by INGREDIENT

Italicized page numbers represent recipe variations.

Almonds 56, 87, 98, 125, 133, 164, 170

Amaretti cookies 168

Anchovies 45, *134*, 150, 182

Apple 60, 95, 153, 163, 170, 180

Apricot 101, 153, 163, 168, 169

Arugula 137, 163

Avocado 92

Baking powder 46, 64, 67, 87, 102, 104, 107, 116, 125, 129, 133, 153, 169

Baking soda 70, 116

Balsamic vinegar 60, 180

Banana 64

Barley 74, 119, 143, *178*

Basmati rice *74*

Bay leaf 167, 178

Beet *43*, 86, 87, *88*, 95

Bell pepper 119, 140, 160

Black rice *74*, 174

Bread 49, 74, 130, 143, 160

Breadcrumbs 115, 164

Broccoli 148

Brussels sprouts *150*

Buckwheat pasta 157

Cabbage 122

Cannellini 74, 115, 122

Capers *43*, 108, 119, 122, 143

Cardamom 125

Carrot *81*, 98, *104*, 107, 148, 178

Cashews 177

Cauliflower *140*, 150, 154

Celery 91, 95, 178

Celery root 154

Chickpea flour 73, 81, 82

Chickpeas 51, 77, 88, 91, 178

Chives *43*, 147

Chocolate 46, 59, *63*, 87, 101, 102, *104*, 110, *133*, 168, 169, 181

Cilantro 125

Cinnamon 107, 116, 125, *153*

Cloves 125

Cocoa powder *67*, 87, 102, 125, *133*

Coconut 56, *102*, 104

Coffee 101, *102*

Cornmeal 45, 46, 51, *67*, 129

Cucumber *43*, 160, 167, 170

Cumin 51, 88

Curry 82

Dates 125

Dill *43*

Edamame 51, *78*, *130*

Egg white *140*

Eggplant 108

Endive 60, 170

Farro 143, 178, 181

Fava beans *130*

Fennel seeds 121

Feta cheese 77, 91, 137, 163, 180

Flour 43, 46, 51, 59, 63, 64, 67, 70, 87, 102, 104, 107, 110, 116, 121, 125, 129, 133, 140, 153, 169

Garlic 88, 164

Ginger *43*, 55, 74, 95, 116, 149, 167

Goat cheese 49, *70*, 78, 119, 130, *180*

Grapefruit *95*

Greek yogurt 98, 119, 133, 154, *160*, 169

Hazelnuts 56, 59, *63*, 67, 101, 107, *133*

Hemp hearts 137

Honey 56, 60, 64, 67, 107, 116, *129*, 163

Leek 55, 70, 73, 149

Lemon 43, 45, 46, 51, 55, 63, 88, 91, 95, 133, 148, 149, 153, 160, 163, 167, 174, 180, 181, 182

Lentils 55, 149, 174

Lettuce 163

Lime 92, *95*, 167

Mango 160, 163, 170

Maple syrup 56, 107

Matcha *46*, 110

Milk 46, 64, 74, 104, 121, 129, 133, 153, 169

Mint 49, 81, 108, 130, 163, 167

Mozzarella *140*

Mozzarella, buffalo *134*

Muscovado sugar 67, 160, 169

Mushrooms 147, *178*

Mustard 43, *170*

Nondairy "milk" 43, 46, 87, 101, 102, *104*, 110, 116, 125, *133*, 169, 181

Nutmeg 116

Oats, rolled 56

Olives 108, 121, 148, *177*, 180, 182

Onion 51, *78*, *88*, 92, 134, 143, 150, 160, 177, 178

Orange 137, 181

Oregano 134, 143, *180*

Paprika 88

Parsley 51, 55, 115, 148, 149, 150, *160*, 174

Pasta, buckwheat 157

Pasta, whole wheat 108, 137, 150, 177

Peach 167

Peas 49, 78, 130

Pepper, bell 119, 140, 160

Piadina 82

Pine nuts 45, 119

Pineapple 95, 170

Pistachios 137

Pizzoccheri 147, 164

Poppy seeds 121

Potato *74*

Potato starch *107*, 133

Pumpkin *70*, *74*, 77, 147

Quartirolo Lombardo cheese *91*, 157, 177

Quinoa 148

Radicchio 60, 177, 180, 182

Raisins 56, 60, 129, 150, 180

Raspberries 63, 64, 133

Rice, black *74*, 174

Rice, semi-polished *181*

Rice flour 46, *59*, *67*, *107*

Ricotta 63, 70, *78*, *108*, *129*, 147, 168

Rolled oats 56

Romanesco *150*

Rosemary 134, 178

Saffron 154

Salmon 137

Shallot 74, 78, 115, 147

Spinach, baby *137*, 157, 160

Spring onion 119

Stevia 153

Strawberries 63, 167

Sugar, muscovado 67, *160*, 169

Sugar, organic powdered 46, 59, *63*, 64, 181

Sun-dried tomatoes 55, 82, *119*, 137, 143, 148, 149, 164, 174, *182*

Sunflower seeds 121

Sweet potato *74*, *81*, 180

Tabasco sauce 160

Tagliatelle noodles 147

Tahini 88

Thyme *70*, 77, 98, 119

Tofu *91*, *98*, *115*, *177*, 182

Tomato paste 108

Tomatoes, sun-dried 55, 82, *119*, 137, 143, 148, 149, 164, 174, *182*

Tuna *43*, 115

Turmeric 43, 51, *104*

Vinegar, apple cider 43, 70

Vinegar, balsamic 60, 180

Walnuts 55, 60, 129, 150, 157, 170, 174

Whole wheat pasta 108, 137, 150, 177

Winter squash *70*, 74, 77, 147

Yeast 121, 140

Yogurt, Greek 98, *119*, 133, 154, *160*, 169

Yogurt, regular 107

Zucchini 78, 81